The problem w̶i̶t̶h̶

is that by the time they are discovered

and developed into training programs,

culture has moved on and

the 'best practices' are no longer 'best.'

What is needed is a learning community

made up of practitioners

who are learning together

in real time.

-Len Sweet

WANT TO JOIN
AN ONGOING CONVERSATION
WITH LEADERS DOING MINISTRY
IN HARD PLACES WORLDWIDE?

JOIN US FOR CONVERSATION,
RESOURCES, AND BEST PRACTICES
AT NEXTWAVE.COMMUNITY.

BOOK ENDORSEMENTS

"Every generation has to rediscover and reimagine the church and its mission. This book will help you do just that. The good news? There are ways of doing church that no one has thought of yet."

Mark Batterson, Author, Lead Pastor,
National Community Church

"Steve Pike has done it again. He brings life experiences, expertise and a rich network of practitioners to provide conversations that will release imaginations on what the church's next level effectiveness looks like."

Doug Clay, General Superintendent,
Assemblies of God, USA

"Steve Pike is dedicated to the preferred future of the church, and it's mission in the world. This book is an insightful, visionary and helpful guide that brings clarity to both heart and mind. Recommended!"

Lead Pastor, Salt Church Norway
Superintendent, Norwegian Pentecostal Movement

"Are you looking for a fresh take on leading new churches into an optimistic future? In Discovering the 21st-Century Church, Steve Pike guides church leaders through the essential paradigm shifts necessary for leadership in our post-Christian culture. Pike doesn't hold back from sharing his insightful personal experiences of leading multiplication movements, and his bent to provide practical tips and tactics is extremely helpful. This book will inspire, challenge, and help you start disciple-making movements that will lead to exponential fruitfulness in the kingdom of God."

**Dr. Ed Love, Director of Church Multiplication
for The Wesleyan Church**

"I love the image of shifting that Steve Pike presents in *Next Wave-Discovering the 21st Century Church*. I learned to drive a car with a manual transmission. To go anywhere, I had to learn how to shift my car into the right gears. So it is with the church. If we are unwilling to learn how to shift our methods with the changing culture, we can quickly get stuck and become irrelevant. Yet if we are willing to shift our methods without comprising our message, we will be positioned to be relevant and fruitful in God's redemptive mission. This book will help any church planter, pastor, and lay leader learn how to shift again."

**Gary P. Rohrmayer
President of Converge MidAmerica
Executive Director of Church Multiplication Partners**

"The beauty of the church is also its tension. It's both fluid but unbending. This wonderful book will help you understand how to plant and cultivate a local 'Bride' that is fitted to Her times"

Scott Hagan, Ph.D.
President, North Central University, Minneapolis, MN.

"The Next Wave delivers a practical framework to navigate strange and uncertain times. Born out of 40+ years of ministerial leadership, Steve Pike ignites prophetic imagination to envision a future for churches in communities across the world."

Dr. David Docusen, author of *Neighborliness: Finding the Beauty of*
God Across Dividing Lines

"If you have a vague sense that church planting in the 21st century needs to be done differently than before but you don't know how, read this book and let Steve Pike, the consummate practitioner/coach, help transform your vague sense into a clear and focused vision."

Andrew Hoffman, urban planter and Executive Director of
ReachNetwork (EFCA

"Our world has been hit by a wave of unprecedented crisis and disruption. Many pastors & churches feel overwhelmed and under-equipped. Some are asking, "How do we join Jesus on His mission in this season?...in the next season?"

If your goal is to be a church that joins Jesus on His mission, then Steve's book will help you ride the next wave rather than be crushed by it."

Alex Rahill, Director of Church Planting,
Evangelical Covenant Church

"Few people help the church think about their thinking better than Steve Pike."

Gene Roncone
District Superintendent
Rocky Mountain Ministry Network

"Steve's instructive and insightful book dives into the next wave of the 21st Century Church, and drawing from the Scriptures and his own experiences, takes a fresh look at the paradigm shifts leaders need to be aware of if we truly desire God's church to grow and multiply. This is a must read book made available at just the right time."

MAJOR WILL DEJESÚS, Corps and Community Mission Director for
Church Planting (The Salvation Army)

"For as long as I have known Steve he has never had his eyes on the "shinny exterior of things." Steve likes to pop the hood open and figure out what makes things go, and then, by asking the right questions, make them go better. This book is a reflection of Steve's curiosity and strategic approach to life and church and his continued pursuit to ensuring that he and those he works with are relevant and effective. Love Steve and love this book. It's a gift to you and your church.

Norm Edwards – The Anser Group, Managing Partner

"Steve Pikes guidance, as a 21st century cultural navigator, provides practical direction for Jesus followers to effectively do gospel mission as they learn to make the necessary shifts to ride this Next Wave"

Bishop Sean O'Neal- California/Nevada Church of God

"It is a special gift to look back at where the church has been, to then look around the corner towards where it is headed, and then see around that corner to the next one. Steve has that gift and takes us on a step by step journey towards where God is leading the Church."

Frank Wooden
Plant SoCal Director
SoCal Network Assemblies of God

"Steve Pike is one of my heroes...a fellow pioneer and a friend. Steve's ministry focus in these days is equipping pioneers called to "the heart of the city". *Next Wave* is written to the pioneers of today. He helps us learn the ways of Jesus so we can translate the Story of Jesus where He sends us. Though Steve has urban ministry in mind, the twelve shifts Steve gives us will work anywhere. As you read Steve's wisdom, let the Spirit show you how to ride His wave where He's sent you."

Dr. Tim Roehl, President/Itinerant Multiplier, Fit & Flourish Network. Author, *TransforMissional Coaching* and *Game Plan: Developing Intentional Missional Ministry*

"If you've ever surfed, you know that not every wave is worth riding and that lulls between sets are normal. The ultimate goal is to ride the best possible wave, get off it before it loses its forward momentum and then paddle back out to prepare to catch the next wave. Pastoral ministry is similar only it has eternal consequences. In this book Steve addresses 12 shifts that will help you (re)learn to read the waves and will encourage you to wait out the lulls."

Dr. Jeffery Portmann
Church Multiplication Network Director

"In the pages of this book, my friend Steve Pike has provided a framework for taking on the challenges and leveraging the opportunities of the 21st century culture."

Scott Wilson, Global Pastor, Oaks Church, Founder of the Father Initiative and Ready Set Grow.

"I have known Steve Pike for 20+ years. His actions as a leader reflect the attitude conveyed in Wayne Gretzky's words when he said, "We skate to where the puck is going to where it is." Steve is a forward thinker. In the church planting world, Steve is a recognized expert in the 20th-century church planting technique. But his new book, "Next Wave: Discovering the 21st Century Church," he shares his groundbreaking discoveries about the nature of effective ministry in the 21st century. This book is a must read for all ministry leaders and aspiring ministry leaders. It is a primer for everyone hoping to multiply disciples in a shifting culture."

J. David McNaughton, Lead Pastor/Entrepreneur

"Reimagining how we do church is no longer just an option for open-minded pastors. It is an essential activity for every pastor. In our culture and rapidly changing ministry context, this book is your guide on how to win at what matters most."

Andy Lehmann- Executive Director, The Father Initiative

NEXT WAVE

DISCOVERING THE 21ST CENTURY CHURCH

STEVE PIKE

FOREWORD BY ALAN HIRSCH

NEXT WAVE

DISCOVERING THE 21ST CENTURY CHURCH

STEVE PIKE

Next Wave
Discovering the 21st Century Church
Steve Pike
ArtSpeak Creative

Published by ArtSpeak Creative, St. Charles, MO

Copyeditor: Kathy Schienle, kschienle@greermarcom.com

Project Management: Davis Creative, DavisCreative.com

Book Design: ArtSpeak Creative, ArtSpeakCreative.com

Publisher's Cataloging-In-Publication Data
(Prepared by The Donohue Group, Inc.)
Names: Pike, Steve, 1956- author. | Hirsch, Alan, 1959 October 24- writer of
    supplementary textual content.
Title: Next wave : discovering the 21st century church / Steve Pike ;
    foreword by Alan Hirsch.
Description: St. Charles, MO : ArtSpeak Creative, [2020]
Identifiers: ISBN 9781736042816 (paperback) | ISBN 9781736042809
    (ebook)
Subjects: LCSH: Christian leadership. | Church work--Social aspects. |
    BISAC: RELIGION / Christian Church / General. | RELIGION / Christian
    Church / Growth. | RELIGION / Leadership.
Classification: LCC BV652.1 .P55 2020 (print) | LCC BV652.1 (ebook) | DDC
    253--dc23

CONTENTS

FOREWORD

by Alan Hirsch

The pandemic of 2020 has obliterated the 20th-century patterns of church and culture. The old familiar church norms are being replaced with a still-evolving new normal. History is speeding up. The inherited 20th-century patterns of doing church and being on Jesus' mission increasingly feel like a wall, not a bridge, to the people we are called to engage. Our culture is "done" with church—and has officially labeled it "non-essential."

For the people of the Church and especially her leaders, this feels like a new crisis, but in reality, the pandemic has enabled us to see the crisis we were already in. The Church is always in a state of crisis—whether we are aware of it or not. Crisis is the Spirit's way of always bringing us back and grounding us in the Jesus of the Gospels—and the Apostolic Genius DNA He continues to lavish on His Church.

In the midst of this crisis, a fresh apostolic movement—focused on Jesus as Lord—is emerging. The marks of this Jesus-centric movement include: a radical community of disciples, centered on the lordship of Jesus, empowered by the Spirit, built squarely on a fivefold ministry, organized around mission where everyone (not just professionals) is considered an empowered agent, and tends to be decentralized in organizational structure.

This Jesus Movement is showing up at the edges and margins of the traditional, organized Church. These called-out leaders often feel like misfits because they themselves are "done" with the traditional 20th-century patterns and culture of church. They are called to hard places and marginalized people. They are incarnating Jesus to people and cultures long overlooked. Incarnational-missional communitas is being experienced in forms that taste like "new wine."

The good news is that as the 20th-century wave has come ashore another wave is forming. A series of waves actually. The incoming waves are the new normal. The incoming waves are learning—or re-learning the ways of Jesus and removing the roadblocks to a Jesus Movement in our midst in the 21st century.

This book you hold in your hands—or on your preferred mobile device— tells the story of those called to the apostolic edge. It tells the story of new patterns, a new normal, and new wine. It tells a story we can find ourselves in. Welcome to the next wave!

INTRODUCTION.

I DIDN'T SEE IT COMING.

I didn't see the wave coming. But all of a sudden, it was breaking, and I was in the impact zone.

I opened my eyes. The red digits of my ceiling projection clock glared at me. 3:40 a.m. Too early to get up. But I knew I would not be going back to sleep. My tired, terrified brain was racing, looking for a solution.

The day before, we'd been informed that the deal fell through on the sale of our house due to a "catastrophic" problem with a wooden support beam that could result in parts of our nearly new house collapsing. As I lay in the dark, the resulting ramifications reverberated through my consciousness. Our carefully earned equity—gone. Our financial security—gone. Our plans for a new organization focused on starting urban churches now in complete disarray.

Up to this point, the journey had looked so promising. Cherri and I met at college. Over our first 12 years of ministry together, we became the parents of two fantastic kids while I served as the youth pastor in three progressively larger churches.

We transitioned out of youth ministry because we sensed that God was calling us to start a new church in Utah. On the surface, this church-planting move seemed a little crazy to our friends and family. But we waded in with confidence, convinced that God was moving us into a new season of ministry. Over the next decade, God allowed us to be a part of the start and growth of an amazing new church in the fascinating state of Utah. Church on the Terrace (now known as "God's Place") grew into a congregation of over 600 and helped to start five other new Utah churches.

Toward the end of our time in Utah, we were invited to move into a full-time church multiplication catalytic role in the Rocky Mountain region. We moved to Colorado Springs and, over the next six years, had the privilege of partnering with the launch of 25 new churches in every imaginable context.

This work at the regional level got the attention of our denomination's national leaders. In 2005, I accepted an invitation to serve as the National Church Planting director for the Assemblies of God.

This new assignment led to the development of what is now known as the Church Multiplication Network. I had the privilege of being the chief strategist for this initiative. But it was truly a team effort. Nine teams of five to 10 leaders each were mobilized to create the initial implementation plan.

In the ensuing years, the Assemblies of God experienced unprecedented expansion in the face of severe cultural headwinds. My "place in the lineup" allowed me to see a big wave coming in—a wave that is both an opportunity and a threat to the missional effectiveness of the Church in America. More about that wave later.

Something else got my attention as well: most new church starts were occurring in suburban communities. At first, I had no problem with that, because suburbs were where most Americans were choosing to live. In fact, the mega-trend in the 1970s and 1980s was migration from city centers to the rapidly growing suburbs. When people left the cities for the suburbs, churches followed them—a smart missional move.

But over the past 25 years, the migration trends have become more complicated. In some metropolitan areas, city neighborhoods have actually grown more rapidly than their suburban counterparts. Almost without exception, city neighborhood populations are growing. But what surprised me was not seeing a corresponding trend in the starting of new churches in urban neighborhoods. More people, less Church. This struck me as unacceptable.

I began to pray about what I should do to address this missional challenge. Slowly, over about a year, Cherri and I began to sense that God was calling us toward a radical shift in focus. We were not thrilled with the consequences of saying "yes" to this shift. It would require us leaving behind my perfectly good career of leading CMN and paddling out into unknown waters, creating a new organization focused on starting churches in city neighborhoods. I was 56 years old at the time—not a good time to reinvent oneself. Adding even more stress to the equation was the fact that despite doing a ton of research, I was unable to find anything close to a "silver bullet" to solve the problem of why the Church was not adequately present in urban communities. I would have to be willing to surf uncharted waters with a board I built myself.

In 2014, we arrived at a point of conviction that this was indeed a step of obedience we needed to take. Contrary to all logic, we submitted our resignation to the Assemblies of God leadership. It was GO time. Our full attention was now focused on solving the urban dilemma.

This NEW adventure has been loaded with surprises. Despite being lifelong ministry veterans, we were surprised by the level of spiritual warfare we have encountered. At one point, our personal financial security appeared to be in serious jeopardy—thus the sleepless night I described in the opening lines of this chapter. We've encountered inexplicable setbacks and challenges. We've attempted a lot of things that just didn't work at all.

But not all the surprises have been unpleasant. Cherri and I decided we would personally need to live in an urban neighborhood setting. We deliberately moved into a high-rise multi-family building in a downtown Denver neighborhood. Our previous residential experiences had all been lived in suburban contexts. We found the difference between our suburban roots and our urban present to be remarkable. We joyfully discovered that we love living in an urban neighborhood.

Some of the surprises have been paradigm-breaking. Concepts that were previously vague notions have now become revolutionary realities for us. We now live in the middle of a phenomenon called "gentrification." We have regular encounters with the people experiencing homelessness who have temporarily chosen our neighborhood as a place to stay for a few days. Sirens blare at all hours. Our neighborhood actually has microphones that listen for gunshots so the police can respond more quickly when there is a problem. Construction cranes dot the city skyline around us. We have one car and sometimes go days without using it. Our new neighborhood friends have diversified faith (or lack of) journeys. Our Zip code leans politically dark blue. When we combine our personal experiences with those of the numerous other urban church starters we've worked with over the past six years, we've directly and indirectly accumulated a treasure trove of urban church-launching knowledge that we—the Urban Islands team—are eager to pass along to whomever is ready to learn.

To date, Urban Islands has assisted 49 church start-up teams in difficult settings. We've partnered with numerous churches, networks, and denominations to help them optimize their efforts to start churches in difficult and urban places.

THE WAVE I DIDN'T SEE COMING.

Here is the unexpected discovery that came out of our efforts to increase the presence of the Church in the city. When I started writing this book, my intention was to help urban church starters go into the urban context more effectively. But the more I wrote—I realized that the insights our leaders were discovering in the urban context are applicable in every church setting everywhere. Why? Because we are all living in the tension between the receding 20th-century wave of culture and the rapidly emerging 21st-century urban cultural wave that will soon be crashing on the shores of every community.

Here's the thing about waves. You have to decide how you will respond to each wave. You basically have three options. Miss them. Be pulverized by them. Or ride them. If you miss them by diving under the wave, you end up in the calm on the other side of the wave going nowhere fast. Being pulverized speaks for itself. Nobody wants to be pulverized. But that's what happens when you choose to stand your ground. Riding the wave requires serious effort that is richly rewarded when the power of the wave grips the board and propels the board and the rider toward the shore.

Here's the thing about riding a wave. You will not finish the ride if you passively stand on the board without constantly shifting your center of gravity. Staying on the wave requires you to intentionally shift to adjust to the constantly changing shape of the wave. You can't stay on the wave without shifting.

My hope is that this book will help you catch the 21st-century urban cultural wave and ride it all the way to the beach! Digesting the contents of this book will help you see the wave that's now arriving, know how to catch it, and understand the shifts you will need to make to ride it all the way to the shore.

TWELVE SHIFTS

The wave is the 21st-century culture emanating from the crucible of the urban context. The shifts are the necessary adjustments we will need to make to ride the wave of the 21st century. The collective learning of the 40+ Urban Islands Project church starts has coalesced into an awareness of Twelve Shifts that leaders must make to effectively ride the 21st-century wave. Here is a brief overview of what the Urban Islands Project cohort is learning about the shifts that will help us all ride the wave:

#1 SHIFT ONE: REDISCOVER THE CHURCH.

From Building the Institution to Catalyzing a Movement.

The sustainable 21st-century church rests on a solid, minimal ecclesiology.

#2 SHIFT TWO: REIMAGINE DISCIPLESHIP.

From Discipleship as a Program to a Lifestyle of Disciple-Making.

The 21st-century church must be built on a platform of broadband discipleship. Start making disciples who make disciples, and the Church will emerge.

#3 SHIFT THREE: REINVENT FUNDING.

From Self-Sustaining to Sustainable.

The sustainable 21st-century church requires a full-spectrum funding strategy.

#4 SHIFT FOUR: RETHINK TEAM-BUILDING.

From Titles and Positions to Communities of Disciples on mission with Jesus.

The sustainable 21st-century church always begins with people first.

#5 SHIFT FIVE: REDEEM ARCHITECTURE.

From Empty Buildings to Fully Utilized Assets.

The sustainable 21st-century church will use architecture creatively.

#6 SHIFT SIX: RECLAIM THE ECOSYSTEM.

From Isolating to Complementing.

The sustainable 21st-century church will participate holistically in the ecosystem of the city.

#7 SHIFT SEVEN: RECALIBRATE THE TIMELINE.

From Launching to Emerging.

The sustainable 21st-century church will respect every formative stage of the emerging church. Discover, Discern, Deploy, Develop, Duplicate.

#8 SHIFT EIGHT: REFRESH THE METRICS.

From Bodies in the Pews to Disciples in the Marketplace.

The sustainable 21st-century church will skillfully measure missional progress utilizing metrics that measure authentic Kingdom advancement.

#9 SHIFT NINE: REFOCUS CHURCH HABITS.

From Calendar Driven to Mission Driven.

The sustainable 21st-century church will embed healthy missional habits into the ongoing rhythms of the church.

#10 SHIFT TEN: RE-CONSIDER CORE VALUES.

From Institution Focused to Mission Oriented.

The sustainable 21st-century church will be guided by core values appropriately informed by 21st-century cultural trends.

#II SHIFT ELEVEN: RECOMMIT TO MULTIPLICATION.

From Addition to Movement.

The sustainable 21st-century church will intentionally cultivate a culture of multiplication that permeates every organizational dimension.

#12 SHIFT TWELVE: REACTIVATE SPIRIT DEPENDENCE.

From Duty to Necessity.

The sustainable 21st-century church will be unashamedly and intentionally dependent on pursuing the ongoing empowerment of the Spirit of God.

All of us will benefit by making these shifts. Now. The recent COVID-19 event has been a wake-up call to the Church. Business as usual will need to cease. We are all living in a new context that demands fresh, Spirit-anointed approaches. These shifts will help us all thrive into the future.

Starting an urban church? I passionately believe that increasing the presence of the Church in the urban context must be a high priority. I believe in increasing the presence of the Church in urban places so much that I blew up my perfectly good job to give all my energy to it. If you are sensing a call to start a new faith community in an urban setting, you will find most of the appendices at the conclusion of the book particularly relevant.

Starting a suburban church? As the suburban culture becomes increasingly infused with the urban worldview, these shifts will help you go where Jesus is taking His Church.

Starting a church in small-town or rural America? We've found rural church starters have more in common with their urban counterparts than they do with their suburban ones.

Reformatting an existing church? Every church built on a 20th-century platform will become increasingly less effective without intentional adaptation. Although this book is written primarily with the leaders of new start-up churches in mind, leaders of existing churches will find making these Twelve Shifts to be crucial for guiding their efforts to keep their church fruitful in the 20th-century culture. I've included an appendix at the conclusion of the book with some specific suggestions for leading an existing church through the Twelve Shifts.

I do not intend to suggest that these shifts provide the ultimate answers to everything or the end of the discussion. The conversation about these shifts is best viewed as a framework for understanding the emerging forms of the 21st-century church. These are some of the shifts we've made on our way toward missional effectiveness in the urban context. The COVID-19 pandemic has accelerated our shared awareness that every place will soon be urban or deeply influenced by urban culture. Understanding these shifts will be helpful for every leader everywhere. Ready?

The wave is here. Enjoy the ride.

SHIFT ONE

REDISCOVER THE CHURCH

From building the institution to catalyzing a movement.

The long shadows of late afternoon drew dark lines across the rapidly disappearing splashes of sunlight. Strings of mini-lights twinkled overhead in anticipation of the moment the shadows completely consumed the sunshine. The delicious aroma of barbeque flirted with taste buds. Laughing children darted in and out of the circles of parents meeting one another for the first time. It could have been any backyard on an early summer evening anywhere. But this one was different.

This backyard contained the families of seven new church leaders preparing to catalyze seven new faith communities in the same city at the same time. Every one of them had left behind vocational stability and ecclesiastical certainty to follow Jesus wherever he would take them. They had moved into their respective neighborhoods and were beginning to lay the foundations of the new faith community they felt called to raise up. Now, they gathered in this backyard, ready to begin an amazing journey together.

Each start-up team would be focused on a specific Denver neighborhood. The diversity was stunning. One team was headed to an underserved community where the predominant first language is Spanish. Another team would be raising up a faith community made up of first-generation immigrants from Africa. Several felt led toward neighborhoods where the majority of residents self-identified as "Nones." One was headed to a part of town that had been primarily abandoned warehouses but was rapidly becoming a favorite millennial destination. A final team was headed toward a gentrifying neighborhood that had historically been mostly populated by African-Americans.

Although the diversity of the group was a blessing, it was also a challenge. Each of the leaders had been through a 20th-century training process designed for starting 20th- century churches. Although some of the training could be adapted, much of it simply did not apply. Because none of us, including me, had been this way before, we would need to discover together the principles that would keep us with Jesus on his mission. We felt like explorers working without a map forging our way through the thick undergrowth one step at a time. We quickly realized that to find our way forward, we would need to pause to define the very essence of what a local church is. Here's what we discovered.

About 2,000 years ago, Jesus began building His Church. The Book of Acts provides us a glimpse of the earliest years of the Church. Church historians pick up the Acts story where Luke left off. The patterns of being the Church were developed in the cultural context of the places where the Church grew. Even though the Acts account demonstrates that the Church originated in the city, over most of Church history, local expressions of the Church primarily served small agrarian communities—because 97 percent of the population lived in small agrarian communities.

Along the way, the church accumulated habits and ways of being the Church that served rural communities well. Local churches became the social centers of small towns and farming communities. They served as the most accessible place to go for education, community problem-solving, and even entertainment. In general, local church leaders were highly respected and a political voice that mattered. When it was time for the members of the local church to gather, they walked, rode horses, or used horse-drawn modes of transportation to the meeting places. In other settings, where the persecuted Church lived, the worship patterns were impacted by the harsh realities of practicing a forbidden faith. Secret meetings in homes or out-of-the-way places became a way of life for faithful followers of Jesus.

While it carries forward some of the basic elements of earlier expressions of the local church, the average "modern" expression of the Church looks very different from church as usual for over 1,800 years.

- Large buildings surrounded by parking lots staffed by brightly coated, smiling parking attendants have replaced small chapels that held fewer than 50 worshippers at a time.

- Attendees driving from far and wide to experience the worship environment that suits them best have replaced village residents walking toward the beckoning bell.

- Carefully crafted sermons expertly delivered by an excellent communicator have replaced thoughtful expositions of scripture passages by a passionate pastor or circuit rider.

- A full schedule of life-stage-based programs designed to help participants incorporate biblical truth into their daily lives has replaced more organic and relational modes of being the Church.

These are just a few of the expectations that modern-day regular churchgoers have when they arrive at their place of worship.

The challenge presented by this most common contemporary form of the local church is that it is increasingly difficult to do in an urban cultural context. Large parking lot? Hard to find and even harder to afford, the closer you get to the core of an urban center. People driving from far and wide? If parking is hard to find, people will choose to drive to places where parking is easy to find. Large buildings? Most available meeting spaces are relatively small (less than 200) or very large (more than 10,000). Excellent communicators? The most gifted orators prefer that their gifts be exercised in the presence of the most people—small crowds of fewer than 200 hardly seem worth the effort. Life-stage programming? Tough to do when the crowds are small.

A major reason that the Church is thinner in dense urban areas is that the most popular forms of being the Church cannot thrive in the urban context. And the problem is only going to get progressively worse as urbanization continues to transform every aspect of every society.

In order for the Church to thrive in the increasingly urbanized future, it will be necessary to get back to the very basics of the core purpose of the Church that Jesus is building. The Church is not a method or model. Big buildings surrounded by parking lots or small secret house church meetings are methods or models of being the Church. Methods and models can and must change. The Church is on a mission—the Mission of Jesus. The mission must NEVER change. It's really important that we do not confuse methods and models with the mission. We need to make sure we are engaging in the Mission of Jesus. Then we can identify the methods and models that will enable the Church to thrive in any context.

SO, WHAT IS THE MISSION OF JESUS?

The story of Jesus interacting with Zacchaeus provides the clearest answer to this question. "For the Son of Man came to seek and to save the lost."1 This statement is reinforced by three parables of Jesus that Luke shares in Chapter 15—the lost sheep, the lost coin, and the lost son. Seeking and saving the lost is why Jesus came. Clear, simple, succinct.

Everything that Jesus did as God incarnate can fit into one of those two categories. Seeking—deliberately connecting with people who are lost—people like Zacchaeus. Saving—deliberately helping His followers grow in His grace and truth. And through His Church, empowered and guided by the Holy Spirit, He continues to seek and save the lost. His Mission—to seek and save the lost—is the mission of the Church. It's that simple and that challenging.

Is it possible that over the years, the simple, clear-cut mission of Jesus has itself become lost in the organizational structures and man made traditions of the church? And is it possible that the confusion over why the Church exists may account for our inability to respond to the missional 21st-century challenge? I believe the answer to both questions is "yes." Too often we've let our models and/or methods be the end in themselves. Instead of asking, does this method or model help us be with Jesus on His mission, we plow ahead with our "best practices," guided by metrics that have little or no connection to the heart of God. More buildings, more noses, and more nickels may indicate that the lost are being sought and saved, but not necessarily. Even more baptisms may indicate we are on mission with Jesus, but upon further review, how many of our baptism numbers are made up of the "found" simply reaffirming their faith?

Yeah but how?

If seeking and saving the lost is the mission of Jesus, and therefore the mission of the Church, how are we to be on mission with Jesus? Jesus answers that question with absolute clarity: "Then Jesus came to them and said, "All authority in heaven and on earth has been given to me. Therefore,

---

1   Luke 19:10 NIV

go and make disciples of all nations, baptizing them in the name of the Father and of the Son and of the Holy Spirit, and teaching them to obey everything I have commanded you. And surely, I am with you always, to the very end of the age."[2] Jesus never said to start church organizations, plant churches, or build church buildings. These are not wrong in themselves, but their existence does not equal being on mission with Jesus. Making disciples is what seeking and saving the lost looks like. This is a root command for the Church. It's what we are individually and collectively commanded to do. "How are we making disciples?" is the basic question for every person, every local church, every church starter and every church organization. For the individual, the question is "How am I making disciples?" For the local church, the question is "How are we making disciples?" For the church starter, the question is "How do we make disciples in this neighborhood?" For church organizations, the question is "How are we equipping the churches we serve to make disciples?"

Seeking and saving the lost is the mission of Jesus and his Church. Making disciples is how that mission is carried out. The Kingdom metric for missional effectiveness is not how many buildings do you own or how many people show up for the weekly worship service or how much money is landing in the offering plate. The Kingdom metric for missional effectiveness is how many disciples are being made.

In the next chapter, we will discuss how to measure disciples being made. The main goal of this chapter is to pause and think about the essence of the Church and the implications for increasing the presence of the Church in every community. If the prime directive of the Church is to make disciples, then the crucial question is not, "How do we start churches?" The key question is "How do we make disciples in this place?" Yet, trying to start more churches is exactly what we keep doing. Guided by 20th-century methods and

2   Matthew 28:18-20 NIV

models formed in the crucible of rural towns and suburbs, we keep trying to do the right thing with strategies that are out of sync with the emerging 21st-century culture. We are confusing methods and models with mission.

Let me explain. I once had a clarifying conversation with the leader of a large American denomination. I asked him if he expected every new church plant affiliated with his denomination to be guided by one particular model or method of planting. He answered by quoting the Chinese leader Deng Xiaoping, who said, "It doesn't matter whether the cat is black or white, as long as it catches mice." I thought I understood what he meant, but just to be sure, I asked him to give me a little more guidance. He smiled and said, "I don't care what methods or models are used as long as disciples are being made."

Exactly. For the Church to be effective in the 21st century, we must start with the question, "How do we make disciples here?" and then seek out the methods and models (if they exist) that will help us effectively make disciples. Due to the unique personalities of many 21st-century communities, existing methods and models may not be helpful. Anointed pioneers will need to discover new methods and models. But the mission will be the same—make disciples.

This chapter is titled "Rediscover the Church" for a reason. The most common western expression of the Church has drifted away from the core disciple-making mission of Jesus and settled for a much less potent institutional identity. To be missionally effective, many aspiring 21st-century church starters will need to let go of methods and models they hold dear and learn how to make disciples in the specific context to which they are called. Letting go of models and methods we are comfortable with is easier said than done. It means holding every piece of our beloved model or method up to the disciple-making standard and asking the question, "How will this help us make disciples in this context?" Only the elements of the model or method that actually lead to disciple-making should be carried forward. Or perhaps entirely new models/methods will need to be developed.

Most likely, to be successful in a 21st-century context, you will need to deconstruct your thoughts about the "essential" elements of the Church before you can build a proactive plan for making disciples. In fact, it is essential that every organization committed to multiplication have a clear minimal ecclesiology—what are the minimum behavioral characteristics that indicate a viable, authentic local church exists? Having worked with thousands of new church starters and leaders of existing churches, I would like to offer a no-frills, minimalist definition of a local expression of the Church that Jesus is building. "A Church is a community of disciples with Jesus on His Mission." I've field-tested this definition over and over and believe it is a helpful starting place for rediscovering the essence of the Church. It was definitely helpful for our seven pioneer church start-up teams.

Let's unpack our minimalist definition of the Church. Notice that, first, the essence of the local church is a community. Jesus said, "By this everyone will know that you are my disciples, if you love one another."[3] Second, the local church is manifested as a community of people who love each other and "do life" together. Third, the membership of the community is disciples—people who are following Jesus and learning to live like Him. Fourth, the community of disciples is actively following Jesus where He leads. Because His mission of seeking and saving the lost continues through his Church, seeking and saving the lost is what the local community of disciples is engaged in. Anything more than a community of disciples with Jesus on His Mission may add to the effectiveness of the local church, but it is not necessary for an authentic local church to be with Jesus on His Mission. When we stay focused on His Mission, His Church is built, and He is glorified.

---

3   John 13:35 NIV

This minimalist definition (or one like it) will be an important asset for any organization desiring to lead their church and/or church organization toward proactive missional effectiveness. This definition is unencumbered by all-too-common trappings and assumptions that slow down the missional progress of the Church. By trappings and assumptions, I mean things like full-time paid clergy, buildings reserved only for worship activities, top-heavy ecclesiastical leadership structures, huge start-up budgets, etc. The 20th-century concept that seemed to imply that all these must be present for the "real" church to exist becomes a drag on the missional momentum of a local church and too often become unnecessary obstructions that stand in the way of rapid multiplication. On average, the 21st-century church will be simpler and more fleet of foot than its 20th-century counterpart. The trend toward less complexity will not be a stylistic adjustment, but rather a deep and comprehensive strategic shift that will enable the 21st-century church to thrive into all the nooks and crannies of culture.

We've seen in this chapter that it's possible our familiarity with favored models and methods may have become an obstacle to effectively increasing the presence of the Church in 21st-century communities. In order to be authentically with Jesus on His Mission, we must be willing to rethink our favored models and methods to ensure that we are indeed following Jesus where He leads. The foundation of being on mission with Jesus is being empowered by the Holy Spirit to make disciples. The next chapter is all about discipleship reimagined.

IN THEIR OWN WORDS...

Matthew and Elora Collver are the founding leaders of The Hills Church, a multi-cultural faith community serving the Park Hill neighborhood of

Denver, Colorado. Here is their story of making the shift from 20th century to 21st century.

"Elora and I spent our early years of ministry at a traditional ministry-driven church in the Dallas area. We weren't a large church by Texas standards, but we did a lot. So much, in fact, that we realized that we didn't know a single person outside of the church in any meaningful capacity, including the neighbors of our two-bedroom duplex. At the time we put the blame for that solely on the overtaxing demands of church life. In hindsight we can see how our own immaturity played just as much a role in our bloated and overcommitted lifestyle.

"So we moved 15 hours away, out of state, away from friends and family, and joined up with a group committed to developing a network of house churches while being nine months pregnant. Seems reasonable! (Boy, we sure did miss our family and old church community that first year of parenting!) We were All In on the organic church movement. It was going to be a grassroots movement that changed the world! We were going to do it right! The truth is, God humbled us...over...and over. Nothing turned out like we planned. For example, at one point, God gave us grace in our failures, and we were able to give grace to expressions of the church that we once held in contempt. Still, there are a lot of good memories from those years. For example, we were able to build friendships with many people who were not interested in Jesus.

"In 2015, we moved to Denver to start a neighborhood church. Our original plan was to live in the neighborhood for a year, then begin weekly public gatherings. However, as the initial official start date drew closer, it became apparent that we were not ready. Those we leaned on for counsel did not pressure us to stick with an arbitrary date. Instead, we waited another full year before launching weekly public gatherings. It was one of the best decisions we've made in this process, as it allowed us to continue to learn the ethos of our neighborhood as well as serve the people of the neighborhood well. (Side note: We were a community of disciples on mission with Jesus before we started Sunday gatherings).

"We've been in and around church our entire lives. We both grew up in pastors' homes. We went to a Christian university and then I went to seminary. The temptation that we are still trying to avoid is coming into the neighborhood and imposing our preconceived ideas of what church should look like—a version of Christian imperialism. From the beginning our desire was to have an indigenous church—native to the neighborhood, homegrown—a church for the neighborhood. When we moved to the neighborhood, our friend and mentor Steve Pike encouraged us not to stand on the street corner and say, 'Let's take this city.' Instead, he said we should be asking how we can serve our neighborhood.

"Full disclosure—we knew very little about our neighborhood when we first moved in, even though we had spent months driving around the city in the time leading up to our move to Denver. So, we devoted ourselves to learning and listening to stories. We want to listen to the people in our neighborhood. We want to hear their stories. We want to know what they are concerned about. What keeps them awake at night worrying? What do they want for the future? What do they want for their kids? How are they trying to justify their own existence?

"To briefly summarize, our neighborhood—like most—is both beautiful and broken. For example, the neighborhood boasts that it was one of the first integrated neighborhoods in the United States. However, the reality is that historically there have been clear divisions between the white, more-affluent part of the neighborhood, and the global majority, less-affluent part of the neighborhood. I could write several pages on that dynamic, as well as how it's personally changed us (including why I used 'global majority' instead of 'minority'!).

"What we learned shaped our strategies and methods. For example, we believe that one of the greatest demonstrations of the power of the Gospel is a church that reflects the diversity of the neighborhood. We take intentional steps to embrace biblical justice, give away power, and promote friendships across racial and economic divides. (That's a truncated picture of what is required.) One example practically is that we share a meal together every fifth Sunday in lieu of our normal worship service. We believe there is no Us/Them division when we break bread together.

"We could not have predicted the story of The Hills Church or our personal story. We are bi-vocational and have been since leaving Texas 13 years ago. That seems normal to us now. We have looked for ways to help our neighborhood flourish and in doing so have developed friendships with people who were working for the good of the neighborhood long before we arrived and will be here long after we're gone (and I plan on retiring here!). God is at work and we're grateful that we get to be a part of it."

SHIFT TWO

REIMAGINE DISCIPLESHIP

From a program to a lifestyle.

Very early on in the start-up process, the leaders of our seven, neighborhood-focused Denver church starts realized they all faced a common problem. The training they had received was largely based on the assumption that most American communities have a decent number of residents with a favorable memory of church in their past. Or, to be brutally honest, they are bored stiff in the church they presently attend. To activate these de-churched, inactive, or bored church people, the strategy taught in almost every church "planting" training event was to make them aware that a new and better church option was available and invite them to be part of making the new church a reality.

The problem our seven urban leaders faced in their neighborhoods of focus was that the number of de-churched and inactive church people with interest was inadequate to support the recommended strategy. We set out to tackle this challenge in our cohort meetings. How do you start a church in a place where no one wants a church to start? Our pursuit of the answer to that question drove us back to our definition of a church. "A community of disciples with Jesus on His Mission." It dawned on us that Jesus never actually commanded his disciples to start churches. His prime directive was that his disciples would make disciples. This command was issued in a context where the majority of the population had no interest or desire to see a church start. The early believers responded to this challenge by making disciples. The secret ingredient that made the early church so potent, enabling them to start vigorous churches everywhere, was that they remained laser-focused on making disciples. Not "planting" churches. The early church emerged out of the process of making disciples who made disciples. With this realization in mind, our seven leaders set out to get discipleship right. We quickly discovered we had some unlearning to do.

Why the need to unlearn? When the average church leader is asked to describe the discipleship process of their church, the answer usually sounds something like this. "We have a four-stage discipleship process. In our 101 class, disciples learn the basics of Christian belief and practice. In 201, they discover their spiritual gifts. In 301, they find their place of ministry. In 401, they are prepared for leadership roles in the church." Something like that. Of course, the persons being discipled are expected to tithe, attend worship services, and participate in other church activities and small group meetings. In summary, discipleship is often viewed as a process that starts with a course or orientation and continues when the course graduates continue to practice regular habits of solid and robust spiritual formation.

Discipleship is almost universally understood to be a process that begins after a person makes a profession of faith. It is assumed that persons being discipled are believers who are growing in the grace and truth of Jesus. In fact, no less an authority than Discipleship.org defines discipleship as "entering into relationships to help people to trust and follow Jesus (Matt. 28:18–20), which includes the whole process from conversion through maturation and multiplication..."[4] Notice the definition clearly indicates that the "whole process" begins with conversion and continues through maturation and multiplication. This view of discipleship is clearly the dominant understanding of the vast majority of churches.

Notice that the most popular understanding of the discipleship process is very clear, intentional, and well defined. It should be so. If discipleship does indeed begin with conversion, then it is important to carefully consider how people are converted, because no converts=no disciples. The conventional answer is that people become converted through evangelism. When asked to describe their evangelism strategies, the most common responses are somewhat fuzzy, sporadic, and experimental, compared to the clarity of their discipleship strategies. The evangelism answer often sounds something like "We do four outreaches a year, participate in three serve events and go door to door once a month." Notice that evangelism tends to be more event driven, harder to measure, and even less personal than the typical discipleship strategies.

In the past, these approaches to evangelism and discipleship have served us well. In the 20th century, when the default spiritual posture of most Americans leaned toward a biblical understanding of Christ and His Church, sporadic evangelism events and outreaches were successful at moving sympathetic but inactive former churchgoers from their couches to the pews and into the discipleship process. Evangelism statistics have

---

4   https://discipleship.org/about-discipleship-org/

tended to be all over the place and tricky to measure. Should we count how many people "raised their hand" for salvation, or how many filled out a "Decision Card," or how many got baptized at the last baptism event?

I heard a joke one time about a study that was done to determine how many people were converted in the previous calendar year. The researchers requested conversion reports from every church and evangelistic organization in the United States. They added up the evangelistic totals from all the churches and evangelistic associations and found that everyone in the United States had been saved two-and-a-half times in the last year. It's just a joke, but it's got a nugget of truth in it. And if we view discipleship as a process that begins at conversion, it's a strategic challenge for the Church. If evangelism is a nebulous, event-driven activity that precedes a very intentional, measurable process we call *discipleship*, then how do we wisely plan our evangelism strategies?

The emerging 21st-century evangelism challenge for the Church is that every day, fewer of the people who live around us lean toward a Biblical understanding of truth. The research group Barna reports, "The U.S. is an increasingly secularized nation made up of increasingly secularized cities."[5] Past assumptions that allowed us to be sloppy about evangelism strategies and still have plenty of people to "disciple" are rapidly disappearing.

Perhaps the most serious problem this presents for the Church occurs when we set out to make disciples in the hard places: urban neighborhoods, crime-infested inner-cities, places made up of marginalized and overlooked people, communities dominated by non-Christian religions and philosophies, etc. If disciple-making cannot begin until a person is converted, how do we make disciples of atheists, gang bangers, and good religious people who

---

5   https://www.barna.com/research-type/infographics/

follow a different path than the way of Jesus? Evangelize them, of course! But how? What events can we possibly concoct that will convince a person to leave the path they are on and go in a completely different direction?

We find ourselves in a dilemma. In the last chapter, we were reminded that the primary mission of Jesus was to seek and save the lost, and the way the mission was to be carried out was through the process of making disciples. How do we square our definition of discipleship with the mission and commands of Jesus? How will we make disciples in the hard places where most people lean away from a biblical worldview?

It's time for us to re-imagine discipleship. It's the prime directive and the key to being on mission with Jesus. It is crucial that we make disciples the Jesus way. A good place to start is by looking at how Jesus made disciples. To begin the process of re-imagining discipleship, let's begin with a couple of really important questions. When were the disciples converted? And when did Jesus start calling them "disciples"?

First, when did the disciples become "Christians"? That's a truly tough question to answer with absolute certainty. Matthew provides the first recorded interaction of Jesus with the men who would become his disciples. "As Jesus was walking beside the Sea of Galilee, he saw two brothers, Simon called Peter and his brother Andrew. They were casting a net into the lake, for they were fishermen. "Come, follow me," Jesus said, "and I will send you out to fish for people." At once they left their nets and followed him. Going on from there, he saw two other brothers, James son of Zebedee and his brother John. They were in a boat with their father Zebedee, preparing their nets. Jesus called them, and immediately they left the boat and their father and followed him."[6] Unless you think dropping their nets and leaving

---

6   Matthew 4:18-22 NIV

boats and families constitutes salvation, then this account does not describe their moment of conversion. But Matthew refers to them as disciples in the next chapter, where he documents the Sermon on the Mount, which answers our second question—"When did Jesus call them disciples?" For Matthew to refer to them as disciples, Jesus had to have already given them the title.

My best guess of when the disciples were actually converted might be the incident recorded in John 20:22, where John writes "And with that he breathed on them and said, "Receive the Holy Spirit."[7] This was after the crucifixion and resurrection but before the ascension and the day of Pentecost. It is possible that they had been with Jesus for three years and he had called them disciples the entire time. I'd like to propose that the making of a disciple begins when a person who is not a converted disciple of Jesus makes contact with someone who is already following Jesus.

It may be that discipleship is a process that begins long before conversion and continues on to maturity and multiplication. I would contend for this viewpoint and add that I believe evangelism happens inside of discipleship.

However, please don't get hung up on this definition of discipleship and miss the point. Even if you disagree with the idea that discipleship begins at first contact, rather than conversion, we can certainly agree that evangelism precedes conversion. Whether you call the pre-conversion phase evangelism or discipleship, effective ministry in our increasingly secular cultural context is going to require a higher degree of pre-conversion intentionality. No more sloppy pre-conversion evangelism/discipleship. We need to become just as intentional on the pre-conversion "seeking" side as we are on the post-conversion "saving" side of spiritual formation.

---

7   John 20:22 NIV

I learned this truth firsthand during the process of starting a new church called The Church on the Terrace in the great state of Utah. Most people know Utah as the state where the vast majority of citizens are members of the Church of Jesus Christ of Latter-Day Saints. Indeed, about 62 percent of Utah residents identify as members of the Mormon Church, which makes it by far the state with the highest population of citizens subscribing to one religious persuasion.[8] In fact, according to The Association of Religion Data Archives, less than 3 percent of Utah residents would self-identify as Evangelical Christians.[9] Needless to say, conventional forms of evangelism that rely heavily on the presence of many inactive and "backslidden" Christians would be completely ineffective in Utah. Active Christians were already committed to the relatively rare existing local churches. If we were going to start a new church made up of people from the harvest, we would need to figure out how to help people move toward faith in Jesus before they actually made a profession of faith. We prayed a lot and did our best to make friends with as many of our neighbors and fellow citizens as possible. We went to every community meeting we could. We participated in community sports leagues. Intuitively, we knew that in order to help someone follow Jesus, they had to know us first. After a couple of years, we rejoiced at the small congregation God was bringing together, many of whom had been far from Christ prior to our efforts to start the new church. We started to wonder if their paths toward Jesus had common elements that could become points of intentionality for us.

We interviewed the people who had come to faith over the past couple of years to see if we could discover the universal elements of their stories.

---

8   https://archive.sltrib.com/article.php?id=1842825&itype=CMSID
9   http://thearda.com/rcms2010/rcms2010a.asp?U=49&T=state&Y=2010&S=Name

Did we ever! What we discovered led me to re-imagine how I thought about making disciples. The principles we discovered about making disciples in Utah are transferable to any missions context in the world. Indeed, we've been guided by these exact principles in our work starting new churches in urban neighborhoods.

Here's what we learned about how people move toward faith in Jesus.

Every person we talked with had made a profession of faith in Christ in the past two years. We asked them to think back to what was happening in their life just before they decided to follow Jesus. They all shared a variety of differing issues that preceded their conversion experience, but the one common element was that they all knew someone who was already following Jesus. Our first takeaway was simple but profound. Every person who came to faith in Jesus had a friendship with someone who was already following Jesus. Every one.

We dug deeper. How did they get to know the friend who was already following Jesus? Most of the time they met them through some common activity, interest, or proximity. They went to the same school, worked at the same place, were members of the same club or sports team, or they were neighbors. A pattern was beginning to emerge. The redemptive friendships started as relationships that formed due to "non-spiritual" activities and endeavors.

Wondering if there was more, we dug a little deeper still. How did the non-spiritual relationships form in the first place? The answer was subtle yet powerful. There was some sort of introduction opportunity so that they learned the name of the person who ended up becoming their friend.

One layer deeper revealed the foundation of the whole process. Before they were introduced, they were positively aware of the person who eventually helped them decide to profess faith in Christ.

Four stages of moving toward faith in Christ began to become clear to us. Four stages of pre-conversion discipleship/evangelism. We named and defined them. Here are the definitions we gave to the different stages, from the perspective of the disciple-maker:

Awareness: A person is aware of you in a positive way.

Connection: A connection exists when you know the name of a person and they know you know their name and you are regularly praying for them.

Relationship: A relationship exists when you know the story of a person and they know that you know their story and you connect with them at least once a month.

Spiritual Conversations: A spiritual conversation occurs when a person you are in relationship with becomes aware that you are following Jesus and that you would like to help them follow Jesus.

In summary, the four pre-conversion stages of discipleship we discovered were: Awareness, Connection, Relationship, and Spiritual Conversations. Each of these stages has a definition formulated in a way that can be measured. For example, the Connection question is "How many people do you know by name, they know you know their name and you are praying for them on a regular basis?" The answer to that question will be a real number. This is important because what gets measured gets done. Think about it. Why do we report how many people show up for the worship service on Sunday? It's one way we can get a sense of our missional progress or lack thereof. Why do we keep track of how many people are in the 101 segment of our discipleship pathway? Again, we want to be able to see the missional progress we are making. We exercise intentionality all the time on the post-conversion side of the disciple-making process. But, too often, our pre-conversion intentionality is sloppy at best.

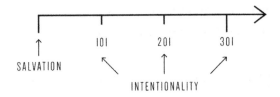

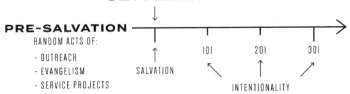

To effectively make disciples, we've got to be intentional about both "seeking" and "saving." This is the mission of Jesus. Seeking and saving is how He is building His Church and He has invited us to be co-laborers with Him. We join with Him in "seeking" on the pre-conversion side of discipleship. We join with Him in "saving" on the post-conversion side of discipleship. The honest truth is that most churches and church people are far more comfortable on the "saving" side of making disciples. In fact, the longer a church exists, the more it tends to emphasize the "saving" side. On the "saving" side, we can keep the subject matter under control. We tend to stay there and are content to be intentional about the "saving" side of discipleship.

WHY "SAVING" SIDE DISCIPLESHIP IS DEVASTATING TO 21ST-CENTURY CHURCH START-UP EFFORTS.

Understanding the full spectrum of discipleship is absolutely crucial for ministry in a challenging context like Utah or in any neighborhood where the number of inactive or dissatisfied Christians is not enough to gather the critical mass necessary to start a new church using 20th-century approaches. If you move into the neighborhood and start activities designed only for the "saving" side of discipleship, you will never get the church off the ground. It will be in danger of becoming one more inward-focused circle of saints, going through the motions of doing church. Your sending organization may be able to count another church start for their annual stats, but the Mission of Jesus will not move forward.

This sets up a dilemma that every church starter faces. The organization that is sending them has invested time, money, and other resources into the start-up team. The sending organization wants to see results and rightfully so. In the 20th century, everyone knew that the metrics are clear and simple. How many noses are seated in the pews and how many nickels are landing in the plate? Because those numbers are tough to count until weekly worship services commence, there is pressure to start holding weekly services.

Who is most likely to show up to a newly announced Christian church worship service? People who are already Christians, of course. Where do these Christians come from? Some will come from other churches, which is irritating to the leaders of the other churches. Others will be inactive or unhappy Christians who have left their previous church and are looking for a new church that "gets it" (and they are the deciders of what "it" is).

Hopefully, some of them have been directly, ethically, and intentionally recruited by the church starter to be part of the "Start Team."

Not knowing what else to do, most church starters give into the pressure and start holding weekly services made up of the aforementioned variety of Christians. In theory, what should happen next is that the pastor of the newly formed church will begin to train the group in principles of evangelism and discipleship. They will go forth and win many souls to Jesus and "badaboom badabam," a thriving church filled with new believers and seasoned saints pops out. Unfortunately, more often than not, that doesn't happen. Instead, the Christians all settle into their usual comfort zones and enjoy worshipping the Lord and having fellowship together with other believers. And the lost are not sought.

This phenomenon is even more devastating in a 21st-century environment because the critical mass of any kind of Christian just isn't there. New churches started on a 20th-century platform tend to have a short life span in a 21st-century context. Organizations grow weary of sending good people to start failing churches in these hard places (where the 21st-century culture is already the dominant worldview) and end up going back to what they know. And the presence of the Church in the hard places (like urban neighborhoods) continues to decline.

HOW TO MAKE DISCIPLES IN THE HARD PLACES.

The solution to this dilemma is simple and extremely difficult. But it can be done. It begins with a broadband strategy for making disciples appropriately in the cultural context. The simple part of this strategy is understanding that in order to have people on the "saving" side of the discipleship journey, you've got to start with people on the "seeking" side. So, start "seeking!" Easy right. The first challenge you will run into is "How do you seek?" The second challenge will be "How do you measure progress?" The answer to both is in our four stages of pre-conversion discipleship.

HOW DO WE SEEK?

1. Phase One—Awareness—Pre-conversion discipleship starts when people are made aware of you in a positive way. Or to put it another way—be intentional about being around people (preferably where they already are) and don't be a jerk! Be kind, thoughtful, and considerate to as many people as you possibly can. It's really that simple.

   The Awareness question for each team member is "How can I make people aware of me in a positive way?"

   The Awareness question for the start-up team is "How can we add value to this community/neighborhood so that our neighbors become aware of us in a positive way?"

2. Phase Two—Connection—Pre-conversion discipleship continues as you interact with people in a winsome way, and opportunities will arise for you to learn their name in a manner that they know that you know their name. Be intentional about meeting people around you by name. Be intentional about remembering their names. And then, be intentional about praying for them on a regular basis. By the way, prayer is not an optional component of making disciples. If you just learn people's names, you will fail. Starting a new church is a spiritual endeavor and a cooperative effort with the One Who is building His Church.

   Praying for the people we meet by name is a powerful action that causes things to happen in the heavenlies. Be sure you don't miss the significance of praying for people "by name." Consider the fact that entire chapters of the Bible are simply lists of people's names. It's strong evidence that God highly values the names of people. We should too. Praying for people by name is a very practical way to do that.

The Connection question for the individual disciple-maker is "How do I learn the names of people I encounter and then pray for them faithfully on a regular basis?"

The Connection question for the start-up team is "How do we intentionally learn the names of people we encounter at events we sponsor or assist with?"

3. Phase Three—Relationship—Pre-conversion discipleship continues as a person moves from being someone you know by name and are praying for to someone who is sharing their story with you and whom you are encountering on a regular basis. Cultivating redemptive relationships creates a platform of trust from which the Gospel can be shared. In most situations, the basis for relationship will not be religious or spiritual in nature. Being in relationship means simply enjoying being with the person you are in relationship with.

The Relationship question for the individual disciple-maker is "How can I cultivate relationships with the people in my life?"

The Relationship question for the start-up or strengthen team is "How do we create or leverage existing opportunities for relationships to form and deepen?

4. Phase Four—Spiritual Conversations—Pre-conversion discipleship continues with spiritual conversations that occur in the context of relationship. With time, the deepening relationship will become a springboard for spiritual conversations that allow the person being discipled to understand how the truth of the Gospel interacts with everyday life.

The Spiritual Conversations question for the individual disciple-maker is "How can I facilitate ongoing spiritual conversations
with my friends who have not yet decided to follow Jesus?"

The Spiritual Conversations question for the start-up team is "How
can we facilitate environments where it is natural for spiritual
conversations to occur?"

HOW DO WE MEASURE OUR MISSIONAL PROGRESS IN THE SEEKING SIDE OF DISCIPLESHIP?

Each of the four pre-conversion discipleship stages we have identified has been precisely defined so that each phase in the process can be
measured just as clearly and accurately as the classic metric "How many
people were in our worship service this morning?"

Measuring awareness: How many people have we made positively
aware of us in the last week? This is actually the hardest metric to get a
"real" number for. The key with this number is to be consistent in what
you count. For example—you may decide to count how many "likes" you
get on Facebook plus how many people you bless with an act of kindness plus how many new Instagram followers you have plus how many
retweets on Twitter plus how many people attended the community association meeting where you made a presentation that was well received.
Your weekly categories to track would be new Facebook likes, new acts of
kindness, new Instagram followers, new Twitter retweets, new community
influence contacts.

Measuring connections: In the last week, how many new people have we
met, learned their names in a way that they gave us permission to know
their names, and we are praying for them on a regular basis? This definition is tangible enough that the result will be a real number.

Measuring relationships: In the last week, how many relationships have been formed as evidenced by the fact that we know their story, and they know we know their story, and we are connecting with them on a regular basis? This definition is tangible enough that the result will be a real number.

Measuring spiritual conversations: In the last week, how many spiritual conversations have we participated in with our friends who do not yet know Jesus? This definition is tangible enough that the result will be a real number.

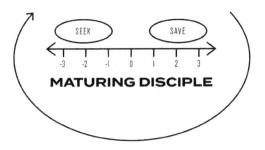

MATURING DISCIPLE

**DISCIPLESHIP
JOURNEY**

DISCIPLESHIP JOURNEY

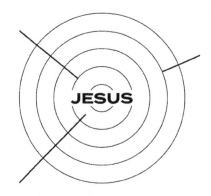

The number of people in each category will be progressively smaller as you move from Awareness to Connections to Relationships to Spiritual Conversations. We refer to this as the Pre-Conversion Discipleship Funnel. The more people who are made positively aware, the more people you will be able to learn their names and pray for them. The more people you are praying for, the more redemptive relationships you will have. The more redemptive relationships you have, the more spiritual conversations you will have. The more spiritual conversations you have, the more people you will assist through the conversion process. The more people you assist through the conversion process, the more people you will be able to lead toward maturity in Christ and the more people will be engaged in making disciples of those around them.

If the 21st-century definition of the Church is "A community of disciples with Jesus on His Mission," then the 21st-century definition of broadband discipleship is "Intentionally, tangibly, and patiently helping those around us walk in the way of Jesus."

Broadband disciple-making is what it is going to take to increase the presence of the Church in our increasingly secularized culture and other contexts where the presence of the Church is thin. Hard-to-reach neighborhoods will never be the same again when start-up teams of committed disciple-makers move into the neighborhood or reformat their existing churches and begin the process of making disciples using a broadband approach. As disciples are made, the institution of the local church will emerge and be invigorated out of the process of making disciples.

Imagine every community blessed with a community of disciples committed to setting in motion a disciple-making movement in that community. Admittedly, it sounds idealistic, especially when the cost of starting thousands of new churches is considered. How will this all be financed? We will take on that question as we explore the next shift.

IN THEIR OWN WORDS....

In 2014, Preston and Lisa Ulmer started the process of catalyzing a new faith community in the Berkeley neighborhood of Denver. Preston now serves as the director of Network Development for the Church Multiplication Network.

What were you doing before you stepped out to start a new church?

Before planting a church, I was a youth pastor, young adult pastor, and a resident director at SAGU.

What did the start-up process look like for you?

We knew we wanted to plant a church for people who were highly skeptical about the faith. It seemed like my education and experiences converged into this type of audience. Since cities were filled with these types of people, we knew we wanted to plant in a major city. Finding a neighborhood happened by walking through the neighborhoods, praying, inviting team members in on the process, and asking people in the neighborhood what type of church they needed.

This chapter is about the shift from a primary focus on the already found to a more balanced focus on the found and the lost. How did that shift happen in your new church start-up journey?

As someone who has been cautious of consumer Christianity most of my adult life, going to a city where there were other "doubters" felt at home. Thinking of discipleship as something that starts pre-conversion didn't feel like a giant shift. The shift for me was how to accommodate Christians who were more conservative in their practices.

What are some other lessons you learned through the start-up process?

Planting a church taught me how to intentionally connect with people like Jesus did. It dismantled any structure I had around the idea of small groups and Bible studies. Innovation and flexibility are the name of the game in the early stages of church planting (and beyond!). With that being said, I wonder if we were too unique at times. Distinctives are important, but I don't want something to be so distinct that it is unrepeatable, or unrecognizable. There is a fine line between leaning into your skill sets and avoiding the other necessary components of a church that don't come naturally. Looking back, I don't think I ever created the proper buy-in with those who were seasoned Christians and who attended our church. In my eyes, they were always peripheral to the mission of seeing the "none of these" come closer to Jesus. I guess that would be my word of advice to the planter who is resilient, adaptable, and thrives in contextualization—figure out how to pastor the 99 so that they are compelled to go after the 1.

SHIFT THREE

REINVENT FUNDING

From self-sustaining to sustainable

"I've got too much money," said no church starter. Ever.

This was a lesson hard learned by the original Denver Seven. One of the Denver churches in particular, which will remain unnamed because of how the story ends, started out so well. The leadership team was recruited around the concept of making disciples who make disciples. Check. The dominant spiritual posture of the average resident in their neighborhood of focus was "none of the above." Check. The initial start-up group were energetic, united, culturally sensitive, and determined. Check. They spent over a year building a relational network with people in the neighborhood. Check. In that year, they were able to help some neighborhood residents move from being a "none of the above" to a "follower of Jesus." Check. Nevertheless, after only a couple of years, the church was forced to close its doors.

The reason? Money. Financial pressures led them to make decisions that caused them to veer off their original mission. Over time, the mission drift caught up with them and ultimately led to their demise. All because they lacked a financial strategy that was built to thrive in the 21st century.

This absolutely heartbreaking post on a Facebook Forum for Church Planters says it all....

"Hey, guys and gals. I could use some prayer. Our Church plant is less than 3 months old and most things are great. People are being saved and we're growing but we're broke. We're reaching a poorer demographic and money just isn't coming in. To be honest the church doesn't even have the money to cover rent this month let alone the rest of the bills. Please pray that God would miraculously provide!"

Stress over money is a real issue that church starters come face to face with sooner or later...usually sooner.

Church-starting organizations tend to approach money with one of three approaches.

Approach 1—The Church Triumphant—Overpower the money problem by generously investing in each approved church start-up at a level that completely removes any question of financial sustainability. The assumption here is that a strongly resourced new church will quickly attract the critical mass of attendees necessary to cover the ongoing operational costs of the church. This approach means that the burden of faith for financial provision is all on the sending organization. The practical outcome of this approach is that the church starter is shielded from having to personally exercise faith. The assumption is that if the starter is unfettered from any financial concerns, he/she will be free to give all of their attention to the work of starting the church.

Approach 2—The Darwinian—The survival of the fittest. The concept with this approach is to encourage the church starter to get out there and exercise their faith muscles, and if they make it through the start-up phase, the organization will step in and help them go to the next level (building acquisition, etc.). In this approach, the burden of faith is all on the church starter.

Approach 3—The Blend—A blend of the first two. The church starter is expected to raise some funds and the sending organization matches or adds to the funds that the church starter raises. This approach means that the burden of faith is shared by the church starter and the sending organization.

The challenge with all three of these conventional approaches to funding is the underlying assumption that adequate operational funds can be raised relatively quickly from the fruit of the harvest. This assumption is reasonable in settings where many of the new attendees will be church members sent out by the sending organization or inactive former church attenders who already live in the community of focus.

But it is a false assumption in most "hard place" neighborhoods, and the further we travel into the 21st century, it will become increasingly rare in every other societal context. Whether the hard place neighborhood is upscale, hipster, low income, gangster, and everything in between, the distance between the commencement of weekly services and adequate tithe and offering income is far greater than what was typical in the 20th-century start-up timeline.

This funding challenge is also a problem for existing churches seeking to reformat their ministry strategies for effectiveness in the 21st century. Existing churches that insist on business as usual will no longer be in business sooner than later.

This is why the approach to raising adequate funding needs to be reinvented for the 21st-century context. We simply cannot rely on the norms of the 20th century to guide us. Investing a lot of money and expecting a quick assemblage of re-activated former church attenders to gather and begin paying the bills is a recipe for disaster. It is an unacceptable waste of Kingdom resources and, even more serious, it is devastating to the church leaders and their families who are being sent on virtual suicide missions. Perhaps even worse, it reinforces the "competitive" nature of multiple churches in the same community because the revenue stream needed to sustain the 20th-century model requires everyone to compete for the same dollars.

Creating a new 21st-century church-funding model will require a significant reset in how we think about financial sustainability for the church. The prevailing funding approaches all assume that once the church is "up and running," tithes and offerings will be the only source of income needed to sustain the church for the long haul. This is not a realistic expectation in the 21st-century context. As we've already noted, 21st-century church costs tend to be higher and 21st-century tithes and offerings income tends to be lower. The reset required is simple and revolutionary at the same time. Going forward, 21st-century church leaders must assume that tithes and offerings will NEVER be adequate to support the ongoing operations of the church.

This assumption will be no surprise to leaders who have been serving in economically challenged communities. Many "mission" churches in tough, "hard scrabble" neighborhoods decided long ago that the offerings they received from their underfunded flock would never be adequate to keep them there. As a result, most, if not all, "inner city" mission-type churches unapologetically depend on a steady stream of support from other churches and organizations from outside their hood who understand the value of what they are doing and are willing to subsidize the mission church income so they can sustain ministry in a place where ministry would otherwise be unsustainable.

The problem with this approach is that it is inadequate to meet the overwhelming need of underserved urban/hard place communities. This means that despite our best efforts to go be with Jesus among the poor, the revenue needed to serve all of the places where subsidized ministry is required will always fall short of the need. We will end up having to triage the neediest, and inevitably, someone will be left out.

At the other end of the spectrum are the upscale, wealthy neighborhoods where the costs are beyond reasonable. The church is not present in these communities for economic reasons as well. One church start-up we know of found that the only space available to rent in their neighborhood of focus was a performance venue that cost the church $4,000 per week to rent. You read that right. Four thousand dollars per week. That's $208,000 per year just to have access to their meeting space three hours a week. Yikes! That amount could be sustainable if the church was able to draw enough tithe-payers to foot the bill, but the venue wasn't big enough to hold an adequate crowd to make the church sustainable on tithes and offerings alone. The church managed to survive about a year and a half but then closed its doors in debt and defeat.

HOW TO HIT THE FINANCIAL RESET BUTTON.

Clearly, the 21st-century environment is hostile to our current church funding strategies, regardless of the unique neighborhood characteristics. All the trends point to a future where this hostile environment will be true for every church everywhere. The good news is that God is not surprised by this trend and He is already guiding His Church to prepare for a different kind of future.

What does that future look like? Having assisted dozens of new urban church starts, we believe we've cracked the code for 21st-century church financial sustainability.

First, we must assume that thriving 21st-century churches will NEVER be sustainable through tithes and offerings alone. Obviously, there will be exceptions to this rule, but it is far better stewardship to assume that tithes and offerings will be inadequate than it is to act as if they will be fine. In fact, we need to make a shift from using the word "self-sustaining" as a descriptor of a healthy church and replace it with the word "sustainable." The most common understanding of the word "self-sustaining" is that a church is able to pay all the bills using tithes and offerings alone. Because, in the near future, most churches will not be able to achieve and maintain the gold standard of "self-sustaining," we appear to be headed toward an era of underfunded churches.

But this unsustainable future is not inevitable. The solution is to replace the concept of "self-sustaining" with "sustainable." Sustainable means that alternative revenue streams are cultivated so that the church is financially viable for the long haul because they are no longer dependent on tithes and offerings alone.

Second, the priority should be on keeping the start-up catalyst (church planter) or the lead pastor of the existing church living and activated in the neighborhood of focus. Without the catalyst, there will be no church. Ensuring that the key leader and family are reasonably provided for is more important than finding a meeting space in the early start-up phase. And as we learned in the COVID crisis, accessibility to meeting space does not necessarily equate to a healthy church. "Reasonably" is a relative term. Some organizations establish a basic salary package for their church leaders that is the same, regardless of context. We suggest that the amount of support necessary be adjusted to match the reasonable livability requirements in the neighborhood of focus. A recommended reference point is that the leader be personally funded at the level of a middle school principal in that neighborhood.

Third, a start-up budget should be developed that will project potential income and expenses for at least five years into the future. In the first phase of the budget period, the majority of funds will go to support the church start-up catalyst family. Later in the budget period, operational costs should be estimated based on the real costs of acquiring the necessary space where church gatherings, meetings, events, etc. can take place. Established churches will need to forecast the financial impact of their expected changes in the way they do ministry.

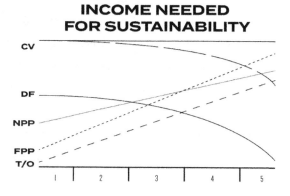

INCOME NEEDED FOR SUSTAINABILITY

Fourth, develop a plan to cultivate and harvest revenue out of five funding streams. The projected revenue from these streams should be predicted in the start-up budget (for a new church) or revised annual budget (for an existing church). This step is really the one that most distinguishes this approach from the 20th-century tithes-and-offerings-based approaches.

THE FIVE FUNDING STREAMS.

Going forward, 21st-century church sustainability will be possible only when all five of the following funding streams are factored in as funding options. The key is to create a diversified "portfolio" of revenue. Not every church will need to harvest revenue out of all five, but it's better to explore every possibility. I've never had a conversation with a ministry leader who told me their greatest problem was that they had too much money to work with. Wise leaders will do their due diligence to explore the potential for revenue in all of these "streams." It will be helpful to think of each of these streams as a category that may include numerous potential options.

1. Tithes and offerings stream: Tithes and offerings will continue to be a funding stream for every church because robust financial stewardship is central to the process of being a healthy follower of Jesus. Simply put, tithes and offerings are a matter of discipleship. Every thriving church will continue to assist their congregants in the practice of biblical stewardship.

2. Donor-based stream: Donor-based giving is a category that includes all manner of giving toward the ministry of the church that is received from individuals and organizations that will never directly be part of the emerging church. This stream can include monthly support from outside donors, monthly and one-time support from sending organizations, and any other financial support that comes from sources other than the local congregation. Sending organizations can support the development of this stream by providing fundraising training and an organizational apparatus that supports receiving donative gifts during the earliest phases of the emergence

of the new church. The potential for donative revenue should not be limited to new churches. Churches undergoing a reformatting process may also discover outside donors who wish to assist them in becoming a more missionally potent church.

3. Co-vocational stream: Traditionally, this stream has been referred to as "bi" vocational. The problem with that term is that it evokes a picture of bifurcation—dividing something in half. Although there are certainly exceptions, it is not generally wise for a person to try to divide their full attention equally between two pursuits that require a high level of attention to be successful. "Co-vocational" refers to the church start-up catalyst or existing church pastor engaging in "compatible" or "complementary" activities that allow the leader adequate time to build the church. Examples might be serving as a Lyft driver or renting out their car through an app like Turo. One of the urban church starters we worked with was able to work co-vocationally by collecting and charging electric scooters overnight. An important factor in this stream is that, if possible, the spouse of the church leader should seriously consider being active in creating revenue. The income generated by the spouse should be factored into the overall revenue accounted for in the new budget.

4. Non-profit partnership stream: Many communities already have a variety of non-profit organizations doing good work in the neighborhood. As a part of the budgeting process, careful research should be conducted to identify the non-profits that are already serving in the neighborhood, and the following questions should be answered: What is their "cause?" What are their physical assets? How are

they funded? Once the church leadership team has documented the non-profits in the neighborhood, they should be evaluated for compatibility and opportunity. It's possible that many of the existing non-profits are already doing some great work in the community that does not need to be reproduced by the church. For example, a well-operated Boys and Girls Club could be a great group to partner with and assist with their programming. This partnership potentially provides a tangible way for the church to add value without a large impact on the budget of the church. It could also be an opportunity to actually reduce costs (which acts like revenue on a balance sheet) by requesting to use space at the Boys and Girls Club facility in exchange for a certain number of volunteer hours. The bottom line is to create a win/win scenario that ultimately benefits both organizations.

Another potential way to generate revenue in the non-profit category is by identifying a gap that no one is filling and creating a ministry strategy to fill that gap. This approach could potentially create positive revenue. For example, a church start-up catalyst we assisted discovered a need for an after-school program in his neighborhood of focus. The start-up team started an after-school program using revenue generated from many supporters who were not interested in assisting with the start-up of the church. But they wanted to see the after-school program happen and were willing to fund that. The church start-up leader created a "parallel" non-profit organization with a separate board and accounting system from the church. He used the after-school program-designated revenue to run the after-school program, which included renting a building 24/7. During the hours the after-school program was not operating, the church rented space for their programs from the after-school non-profit for a very affordable price. In this way, the church dramatically lowered their facility costs, while at the same time providing a very needed service to the community.

5. For-profit partnership stream: The dense population of many urban neighborhoods allows for the emergence of many local small businesses that provide desired goods and services for the local residents at reasonable cost. In fact, many urban neighborhoods actually reject the insertion of chain stores into their hood. "Work local" and "buy local" are strong sentiments in many urban communities. It is realistic, then, to consider the possibility of funding some of the costs of "doing church" through for-profit efforts. One of my favorite examples of this approach is One Reason Church in Minneapolis, Minnesota. The pastor, José Perez, grew up in the nation of Venezuela, where he became a professional dance instructor. He eventually became the owner of a dance studio and ended up owning a chain of dance studios across the nation of Venezuela. He met Jenna (an American who went to Venezuela as a Christian missionary), who eventually became his wife, and through her patient influence, started following Jesus. The couple moved to the U.S. and began serving as staff pastors in a local church. They sensed God calling them to move to Minneapolis to start a church. But José knew that funding the new church would be a challenge. After considering his options, he realized that people in his neighborhood of focus needed access to a dance studio. Responding to the need, Jose and Jenna started One

Reason Dance Studio first, and months later they started One Reason Church. The dance studio covers the cost of facility rental and the church provides a great foundation for the personal support of José and Jenna, along with the operating expenses of the church. Not a dancer? Don't be discouraged. Other for-profit possibilities are out there. Coffee shop churches, event centers, daycare, etc. are just a few of the possibilities for creating revenue to support the emergence of a new church.

Before a church makes an irrevocable commitment or takes irreversible actions to start or reformat a church, their governing organization should request a comprehensive five-year ministry plan that forecasts the expected expenses and demonstrates how the church will harvest revenue out of all five revenue streams. Every story will be different. Every situation will have different obstacles and opportunities. Every church leadership team will bring different assets and liabilities to this process. Every ministry plan will be unique.

Creating this extensive and well-thought-out ministry plan is a great way for a church starter to "count the cost" before they move their family into a stressful situation. It is a much-needed step in the process of wisely reformatting an existing church. Obviously, the ministry plan is only a plan and it is unlikely that any of the details will play out exactly as the church starter has predicted. But, the process of creating the ministry plan will provide the church with wonderful opportunities to come face to face with the realities of what they are proposing to do and empower them to discover creative solutions before the lack of finances sabotages their missional efforts.

The best of these ministry plans will make tithe and offering income an added blessing on top of the income produced by the other revenue streams. The side benefit of this approach is that the church will no longer be dependent on the "fruit of the harvest" for the financial stability of the church. Instead of being incentivized to pursue people who already understand Christian stewardship principles, a lack of total dependence on tithes and offerings allows the church starter to give appropriate attention to seeking and saving those who are lost.

In this chapter, we've discovered a fresh and holistic way of thinking about the funding strategy for churches. Sooner than later, financial strategies for churches, regardless of their context, will need to be modified to respond to new financial realities that will put unprecedented pressure on every church. Author and Pastor Mark DeYmaz has written an excellent book, *The Coming Revolution in Church Economics*, that will help you think through the implications of this challenging new playing field. Another important book on this topic is *Church for Monday*, by Dr. Svetlana Papazov. Both of these books should be required reading for anyone who aspires to start a new church or reformat an existing one.

Having considered an effective strategy for properly approaching the funding of churches, the next shift will focus on gathering the team needed to lead the church into a thriving missional future.

IN THEIR OWN WORDS...

This chapter has highlighted the need for a revolution in ecclesiastical financing.

Michael and Svetlana Papazov, founding leaders of Real Life Church in Midlothian, Virginia, are pioneering creative solutions to the new church financing puzzle. Here's a brief overview of their story.

"In order to close the Sunday-to-Monday gap between church and the marketplace in a way that would allow us to duplicate a model of an entrepreneurial church, my husband Michael and I, with a team of supporters, started Real Life Church in Midlothian, Virginia (https://www. reallifechurchrva.org/). We desired to embed ourselves in the economy of our city to reach business owners and entrepreneurs and bridge the sacred and secular divide in a practical way.

"Working primarily among unchurched demographics required a new way of thinking about funding the church start-up if we were to become sustainable for the long haul. Church planting, as any other start-up, is difficult and hallmarked by an enormously high rate of failure. If we were to put all of our eggs in one basket, it almost would have spelled a disaster. We couldn't rely exclusively on the tithes and offerings of brand-new Christians and pre-believers or even the funding support of church planting organizations. In order to set up our church for thriving, we had to create a diversified 'portfolio' of revenue that, in addition to donations, and tithes and offerings, would include for-profit and non-profit streams.

"Shortly after launching Real Life Church, we opened Real Life Center for Entrepreneurial and Leadership Excellence—a non-profit business incubator that prepares people for their occupations. Both of these 501(c)3 entities operate from the same location, since the church's activities happen on days and times when the incubator is not busy. The entrepreneurial center generates revenue for the church through leasing private offices and facilitating business training, entrepreneurial meet-ups, workshops, and networking events. In addition, I am co-vocational and generate income not only as lead pastor but also as a coach and business consultant at Real Life's entrepreneurial center. This funding model has allowed us to simultaneously be fulfilling the mission of Real Life Church in the market-place and become sustainable.

"Hundreds of adult entrepreneurs have been trained at Real Life through workshops, masterminds, business coaching, networking, and caring relationships. The Entrepreneurial Center trains in leadership and entre-preneurship to give unchurched people the opportunity to experience God and faith outside of Sunday as we lift our community economically, socially, and spiritually. We care for our community and contribute to our local economy by guiding people to identify and develop their gifts and skills in order to lead well at their jobs, hire new employees, or start new businesses. We do business incubation, offer co-working space and private offices for work, business consulting, networking to identify new job opportunities, educational workshops, and adult and next-generation entrepreneurial training. Most of these functions are facilitated by church volunteers skilled to equip in these various ways.

"We have found that developing people's entrepreneurial skills sets them up for success and unleashes their potential. Having a problem-solving mentality, with a growth-oriented mindset, one can do well anywhere: at home, at school, at work, in government, and in business. For that reason, we have created faith and entrepreneurship programs for kids, teens, and adults. The programs of Real Life KidPreneurs and Real Life TeenPreneurs as summer camps, Beyond VBS, and school classroom curricula have been effective in fostering next-generation creativity. The Real Life AdultPreneurs program trains in business and entrepreneurial skills for adults interested in starting their own businesses and also for those affected by the opioid crisis and at-risk situations. During our Kid-, Teen-, and AdultPreneurs programs, we encourage people to dream, create, and contribute.

"Although our real estate has a small footprint, we believe we can make a big difference with it. Real Life's small building of 3,200 square feet has provided co-working space and offices for more than a dozen businesses. One such business owner is Pam, a financial professional who came to us when she couldn't afford her own building. The local coffee shops no longer fit her clients' needs. She was in that in-between stage where many entrepreneurs do not make it. The Real Life incubator supports entrepreneurs by offering private offices in vulnerable times of too-fast-growth and not-enough-capacity. In our facilities and in our programs, Pam has found a place to belong, grow, and steward hundreds of thousands of dollars for her clients. She has hired four employees, and her impact on the economy has increased because Real Life supports small business owners with entrepreneurial environments and low-cost rent.

"In addition to offering private offices, we facilitate business training based on Biblical principles. Hundreds of adult entrepreneurs have been trained at Real Life through workshops, masterminds, business coaching, networking, and caring relationships. In this way, we empower for greater contribution to our local economy.

"Moreover, we have unleashed the imaginations of hundreds of children through the Real Life KidPreneurs and TeenPreneurs programs. Spurred into creativity, Zoe and her older sister, Chloe, launched a small business called Knicks and Knacks after finishing the Real Life KidPreneurs summer camp. Together, they have developed a line of goods with teens and preteens in mind. These are two young entrepreneurs who are not waiting to become adults in order to dream, create, and contribute to our local economy. In all of our training, we focus on developing an entrepreneurial mindset with a biblical worldview. We teach that business dreams can have a social and economic impact on the real world and the real economy. We help adults and kids reverse-engineer their dreams into strategic business plans that they can launch now.

"The majority of the people in our church start-up have joined because of faith and entrepreneurship integration. Kelly, a digital marketing expert, re-connected to God and faith and is now a committed member of our church because she was looking for a space to expand her business and rented an office at Real Life. Liza came to our Christmas Small Business Open House Expo as a vendor. The next Sunday she came to church and recommitted her life to Christ. Now her kids, too, have become a part of the church. Terry is a freelance photographer who one Sunday came on our property to take pictures of his client. As my husband and I approached him, he thought he would get in trouble because of trespassing. To his surprise, we welcomed him to utilize not just the outside of our property, but the business incubator as well, by doing photoshoots in one of our vacant offices. That deeply impacted him, and Terry and his wife came back to Real Life, this time to church, and there they found a genuine church family that has welcomed them home. Terry's photography business has also expanded since joining our Real Life church community. These are only a few of the many lives that have been touched through Real Life's integration of faith and entrepreneurship."10

10   Excerpted from *Church for Monday: Equipping Believers for Mission at Work* by Svetlana Papazov (Living Parables Books, 2019). Available everywhere print books are sold. Excerpt used by permission of Living Parables Books/EABooks Publishing, 1567 Thornhill Circle, Oviedo, FL 32765 https://www.eabookspublishing.com

SHIFT FOUR

RETHINK TEAM-BUILDING

From titled positions to disciples on a mission.

The idyllic environment of the backyard barbeque had become a distant memory. All seven leaders of the seven new Denver church start-ups were now slogging through the grind of the start-up process. Money pressures were rearing their ugly head. The idealistic concept of making disciples who make disciples was crashing painfully into the reality of how hard that is to do. The ambiguity of the start-up process was taking its toll on the mental and emotional health of everybody. But one factor began to emerge as an early indicator of missional success—the ability of the starters to recruit and activate a solid team optimized for the 21st century.

Recruiting and building a team is a fundamental leadership practice and was always a significant component of 20th-century start-up strategies, as illustrated by the confident young church starter who introduced himself to me at a conference where I was the keynote speaker. He proudly told me he was starting a church. Then he turned to a group of people behind him and said, "Let me introduce you to our team." He proceeded to share the names and titles of about 10 people. "This is our youth pastor. This is our children's pastor. This is our worship pastor. This is our creative arts pastor." Etc. Each and every team member had a title that implied some sort of responsibility over an aspect of one of the ministries of the church. I assumed this was one of those outlier churches that had quickly grown and required the staff to grow quickly as well. "Tell me about this church," I inquired. "Well, we expect to launch weekly services in the fall," the confident lead starter replied.

The dialogue above is a classic illustration of the team-building approach of the 20th century. The common language used for the team described above was the "Launch Team." A major time and energy focus of the "Launch Team" was the upcoming commencement of weekly services. Like the example above, it was not uncommon for every member of the "Launch Team" to have a title and responsibility that was centered around making the weekly worship gathering spectacular. Team members were selected for their skills at leading and participating in really good worship experiences and the supporting activities like children's ministry, parking lot attendants, etc. Community engagement was encouraged but revolved mainly around inviting people to pre-launch gatherings and the actual launch itself.

The underlying assumption that led to this type of team-building was that the key to a successful church launch was an outstanding worship experience. Well-respected proponents of the 20th-century approach to team-building have said things like "It's all about Sunday" or "Your job is to bring them and our job is to win them." The reason this approach was common and usually successful was because most 20th-century Americans had a favorable memory of their engagement with church as a child and perhaps even a procrastinated intention to get back into church at some point. The invitation to a church worship service was generally viewed as a good thing to go be part of. In this environment, he who has the best worship service wins.

The 21st century has obliterated this assumption. A 2019 report by The Unstuck Group indicates that "Churches have a 'front door' challenge to overcome. For churches to maintain health and growth over time, the number of first-time guests over a 12-month period needs to be equal to or greater than their average weekly attendance."[11] That's way easier said than done. So-called "Nones" (individuals who identify as having no religious interest) are the fastest-growing category of religious behavior. This recent headline on Religion News Service says it all... "'Nones' now as big as evangelicals, Catholics in the U.S."[12] A large segment of the population is running away from "organized religion" and the excellence of our worship gatherings is no match for their determination to put God in their rearview mirror. As the number of "Nones" continues to expand, the approach to church that assumes it's all about the worship service will become less and less effective at helping people far from God find Him.

A new kind of team-building is needed to effectively start and reformat churches optimized for the 21st century. The 20th century was built on the assumption that the culture in general contained enough people with a favorable memory of the church to create the critical mass for a strong launch of a better version of their memory.

---

11   https://theunstuckgroup.com
12   https://religionnews.com/2019/03/21/
nones-now-as-big-as-evangelicals-catholics-in-the-us/

In this chapter, you will discover how to cultivate and build the teams you will need to start or reformat a church for the 21st century. You will discover how to increase your team member candidate pool, how to invite team members into the vision for the future and how to keep your teams healthy for the long haul.

The foundational assumptions of the effective 21st-century church must be built on a different set of assumptions than its 20th-century counterpart.

ASSUMPTIONS FOR THE EFFECTIVE 21ST-CENTURY CHURCH.

Assumption #1: God is our source. Without intending it, the 20th-century approach to team-building was based on the idea that tithers in the pews were what we needed most. Of course, our language indicated our dependence on God, but our actions belied our real source of security. 21st-century team-building is constructed on a platform of complete reliance on God. He is the Source. His is the mission—to seek and save the lost. He is already at work in the community He has called us to. He is more interested in our spiritual formation and participation in His mission than He is in us being the fastest-growing church in the city, state, nation or world. Because it's all about Him, He will provide everything we need to carry out His will and purpose for us and the people around us.

Assumption #2: People are the conduit of His provision. 20th-century team-building mindsets unintentionally turned people into a means to an end. To get tithers in the pews, we needed skilled worship providers on our team, so money from experienced tithers could land in the plate, so we could pay the skilled worship providers, light bills, and mortgage payments on the building. Our view of people inadvertently turned being a church into a vicious cycle of attracting people so we could afford to pay for everything we used to attract them. Ironically, when we see people as the source, we start depending on them for everything instead of looking to the Lord, and before we know it, the tail is wagging the dog. We can't afford to disappoint our source, so we ask them what they want and do everything we can to give it to them. Before we know it, we are following the will of the people instead of the will of God.

21st-century team-building views people as the conduit of God's provision. He is the source. Period. But He invites us all to be conduits of His provision. Whether we are talking finances or team members, this is how things work in the Kingdom of God. Everything needed to start or reformat a church will come from the Lord through, not from, people.

Shifting from "from people" to "through people" is crucial for effective 21st-century team-building. Why? Because when you view God's provision as coming "from" people, then you are limited by what the people have to offer. But when you view God's provision as coming "through" people, then your only limitations are what God wants to provide. And He will always give abundantly to those who are focused on His mission.

Assumption #3: Recognizing that God is the source and people are the conduit will dramatically impact the way we build teams. Instead of looking for people who can skillfully do ministry things, we look for people who are willing and able to join Jesus on His mission—to seek and save that which is lost. We look for people who are disciple-makers or at least willing to become disciple-makers. As we've already stated in this book, making disciples is what Jesus actually commanded us to do. He never commanded us to start churches. He told us to make disciples. 21st-century team-builders focus on building a team of disciple-makers first and then trust God to provide everything they need (skilled worship leaders, money, etc.) through the disciples who are being made.

Pause for a minute to reflect again on these words. "God is our source. People are the conduit of His provision." The fact that God is our source must never become a mere theological concept we give intellectual assent to. 21st-century church leaders must actually believe this is true. God is the one and only source we look to for everything we need. Money, buildings, resources, and people. 21st-century church leaders must lean completely and wholeheartedly on God.

But the equally true complementary idea is that people are God's conduit for His provision of everything we need. Yes, it's true that Peter caught a fish with money in its mouth, but that's the exception to the norm. The normal way that money and resources are provided for Kingdom purposes is through people. People obey God and give tithes and offerings. People start businesses and the businesses provide jobs, the jobs provide income, and the income empowers people to obey and give to the furtherance of His Kingdom. Buildings are built by people using materials that God has created. Resources are shared by people using assets they have acquired with God-given gifts and abilities. The greatest need of every church starter is—People. Specifically, people who are disciples and disciple-makers.

Your ability to build a team of disciple-makers is also a crucial "leading success indicator" of your ability to effectively catalyze a new community of faith. We have observed that a strong correlation exists between the number of team members you are able to activate and the number of people who will become part of the emerging faith community. A good rule of thumb is that the number of committed team members will be equal to about 20 percent of the average number of people who gather together when you begin holding regular public gatherings. For example, a new church that typically gathers 100 people for worship will be supported by about 20 committed team members. If you are unable to rally committed team members around the vision of the new church, you will ultimately struggle to start a strong, sustainable community of disciples. It is impossible to over-emphasize how critical the matter of team-building is. Just like your financial sustainability strategy, your team-building strategy must be started very early in the start-up process and continue to be a high priority throughout. You will be tempted to lean heavily on mass advertising, social media, and other impersonal forms of team-building. Do not take that bait. Much of your early energy should be directed toward cultivating a solid, united start-up team with as many active members as you can possibly recruit.

21st-century team members will be recruited to a different purpose than 20th-century team members. 20th-century team members were valued for their ministry skills and even their ability to give financially. 21st-century team members are valued for their relational and disciple-making skills. The most important work of the start-up team will be directly engaging with people in the community. 20th-century team members received their titles first and then jumped into action. 21st-century team members will start with action and receive their titles later. And the action they jump into will be connecting with people, building relationships, and helping the people they connect with move toward a saving knowledge of Jesus.

HOW TO EXPAND YOUR PEOPLE RESOURCES IN THE 21ST CENTURY.

God is not surprised that you are leading the start-up process of a church. He's known about this since before you were born. All through your life,

He's been preparing you for what you are now doing. A key provision of His preparation has been the people He has brought into your life.

Stop and think about your life—your childhood years, your time as a teenager, college/vocational training years, your early career, all the way up to the present. Think about the people you've met during all those phases of your life and then pause to consider this thought from King David "Your eyes saw my unformed body; all the days ordained for me were written in your book before one of them came to be." Every day was written down in advance and has played out according to His purposes. Indeed, some of these memories will bring pain or regret. Others will be pleasant and a blessing to reflect on. Good, bad, or ugly, every day contained something that has the potential to provide what you need the most right now—people.

Each of those people that God has brought across your path has the potential of being a part of His provision for the challenge that lies before you. Some will be prayer partners. Others will be financial supporters. Others will be sage advisors and coaches. Still others will be called to walk directly with you as a contemporary colleague in the process of starting a church for the 21st century. How do you tap into this amazing reservoir of provision that God has brought into your life? Here are some recommended action steps for discovering the wealth of people resources that God has brought into your life.

1. Make a list of everyone you have ever known. That's right, everyone, regardless of whether you think they can be helpful to you or not. Even people you might consider to be anti-God or anti-church. If you know them, whether that contact is positive, negative, or neutral, they should be on your list. Online social networks like Facebook, etc.

can be a huge help in this task. Make the list as exhaustive as possible. God has already generously provided through all kinds of conduits. If you are married, your spouse can help you with this process and make a list of their own, so that the extent of your relational network is as comprehensive as it possibly can be. Think in terms of hundreds of names. Keep digging into your memory and your social networking tools.

2. Pray over the list. Pray over each name on the list and listen to what God speaks to you about each person as you pray for them. You may feel prompted by the Spirit to reach out to specific people for definite reasons. Others you will simply have the privilege of lifting before the Lord and asking Him to bless them with His power and presence. As you pray, make notes next to names that the Spirit speaks to you about.

3. Prayerfully categorize the list. To successfully start or reformat a prevailing church for the 21st century, you will need to build at least the following teams: A prayer team, an advisory/legal team, a financial support team, a start team, and a lead team. Depending on your context, you may see the need for other teams to be formed. Now, as you prayerfully go through the list, think about how the different "conduits" on your list might be able to contribute to the process of starting a 21st-century church.

4. Pause and look at your list of teams and the potential members you've listed for each team. This is a good time to ask yourself if you've included enough diversity on the teams where diversity is crucial for success. Truth is that we all tend to want to be on teams

with people who are just like us. But it's been demonstrated over and over again that the healthiest teams are built with people who see things differently. In an article entitled "Why Diverse Teams are Smarter," published in 2016, Harvard Business Review authors David Rock and Heidi Grant conclude that diverse teams "focus more on facts," "process the facts more carefully," and are "more innovative" than teams made up of people with similar backgrounds and perspectives.13 While ethnic, gender, and cultural diversity are the most obvious distinctions to consider, personality types, spiritual giftedness, and the APEST (Apostles, Prophets, Evangelists, Shepherds, and Teachers)14 grid should be considered as well. The teams you build will be better when you include a variety of ways of seeing the world.

INVITING PEOPLE TO JOIN YOUR TEAMS.

Once you've categorized the names on your list (it's very possible that a person may be on more than one team), it's time to plan your invitation strategy. Think carefully about what it will require of you to manage and communicate well with each member of each team. Think about what you actually need each member of each team to do. How much of their time are you asking for? How long are you expecting them to commit to be part of the team? Why is this team essential to the success of the start-up process of the church? What is the big-picture vision you are inviting them to be part of?

Answer all these questions before you begin reaching out to people to invite them to be part of any team. Obviously, some of these teams require a higher level of commitment and involvement than others. Your strategy for inviting participation should reflect the level of commitment you will

---

13   https://hbr.org/2016/11/why-diverse-teams-are-smarter
14   https://www.theforgottenways.org/what-is-apest.aspx

need from the invitee. For example, while it may be acceptable to send out a general email invitation for people to participate on your prayer team, it will be wise to invite your prayer team leaders and your strongest intercessors through a personal, preferably face-to-face, invitation. Likewise, appeals for general financial participation can be made through email and social media, but your strongest financial supporters will be individuals with whom you've had a face-to-face opportunity to invite their investment into the vision.

When inviting people to be a part of your start team, it is crucial that you clearly describe to them what you will be expecting of them. Too many church start teams are sabotaged by expectations that are out of alignment. If they think you are inviting them to show up for the first service and you think you are inviting them to be part of a disciple-making movement 12 months in advance of the first service, you are both going to be frustrated with what happens next.

After you've categorized your list and determined your expectations for each category, it's time to invite the people that God has brought into your life to join you in starting the church. For the most crucial positions, face to face is the only way to go. Help them understand why the church you are starting needs to succeed and then ask them to join you in a specific way, with your expectations clearly explained. They also deserve a clear understanding of how long you are asking them to commit to being part of the team.

Team-building should begin very early in the process of starting the church. Well-built teams will make a huge difference in the effectiveness of the start-up process. The cliché "teamwork makes the dream work" applies here.

KEY TEAMS TO CONSIDER.

This is a non-exhaustive list of teams you may consider building as you lead the start or reformat process of a church.

Prayer Team.

Your prayer team should be as big and broad as you can make it. The great thing about prayer is that people who will never attend the church you are starting can be a part of your prayer team. You may want to consider at least two levels of prayer engagement.

Level One: General Prayer Partners who agree to add you to their prayer list and pray for you on a regular basis. You should plan to communicate with your General Prayer Partners via a regular form of communication like an e-newsletter.

Level Two: Prayer Warriors whom you recruit face to face and meet with face to face (or perhaps via a video conferencing tool like FaceTime or Zoom). These will be people who are recruited specifically because you know they are people who know how to intercede and who have embedded prayer into the rhythms of their life.

Financial Support Team.

Like your prayer team, your financial support team should be large and diverse. In fact, a diversified financial support team is crucial for the long-term sustainability of the new church. Several factors should be considered when you recruit your financial support team.

Factor One: Make it as easy as possible for potential team members to be a conduit of God's provision in their preferred manner. Some may prefer to give one significant (for them) financial gift. Others prefer to give a series of smaller gifts monthly. Others may have property they desire to donate. Support those who support the cause of starting by making it easy for them to channel God's blessings.

Factor Two: Although every financial team member should be a financial contributor, some will be able to contribute far more in knowledge and experience. In fact, you may want to specifically recruit financial team members to oversee each of the five funding streams suggested in the chapter on money.

Factor Three: Practice good communication habits with your financial support team members. Say "Thank You" a lot. Frequently help them see how their investment is making a difference in specific, compelling ways. General monthly givers can be thanked via a regular e-newsletter or other online tool. High-capacity donors should be thanked face to face as often as possible.

Factor Four: Always be building your financial support team. Remember, you are not raising money for you. You are raising money to fund the Mission of God in your specific community. This is not all about you. It's all about Him.

Factor Five: Constantly adding new financial team members is important because others will be dropping off. When you have a habit of adding new members to this team, it will be much easier to be gracious when donors discontinue their support. It always hurts when you lose a supporter, but knowing that others are joining the team will soften the blow and help you avoid showing your disappointment.

START TEAM/GUIDING COALITION.

In a new church, it's called a start team. In an existing church, it's called a guiding coalition. Team members on this team are committed to the vision almost as much as you are. They understand the mission and they are willing to give time, money, and effort to help the vision become a reality and the mission to be accomplished. They are personally engaged in building the necessary relational network. This is the team that will have the most visible impact on your effort to start or reformat a church. This team is where the 20 percent rule applies—in a church start-up, if you are hoping for a solid community of 100 people to form, you will need 20 start team members. In a church reformat, if you are hoping for 100 new people to be welcomed into the church community, you will need a guiding coalition of 20. Start team/guiding coalition team members will all be fully engaged in building the relational network we discuss in the chapter on reimagining discipleship. Unlike prayer team and financial support team members, start team/guiding coalition team members must be part of the actual worshipping community, because most of the actual ministry of the church will happen through them. In their book, How to Change Your Church Without Killing It, Jim Mellado, Alan Nelson, and Gene Appel have some very helpful insights for reformatters on the concept of a guiding coalition.[15]

LOGISTICS TEAM.

These are good-hearted folks who have special skills that will enable the church to do whatever needs to be done. Technical support, administrative support, accounting services, manual support of mercy ministries, etc.

OPERATIONS TEAM.

Members of the operations team oversee specific areas of responsibility like the ministries to children, crafting the worship experience, coordinating community volunteer efforts, leading the youth group, etc. Members

---

15   https://books.google.com/books/about/How_to_Change_Your_Church_Without_Killin.html?id=PU59PgAACAAJ

of the operations team should be recruited out of the start team/guiding coalition after they have proven themselves to be behaviorally committed to the vision, mission, and values of the emerging church.

You will likely find it necessary to develop other teams that fit the reality of your specific situation. Building effective, committed teams is essential to the ongoing health and sustainability of any new church. If you are unable to build effective teams, you very likely will be unable to lead an effective church.

The dominant leadership model of the 20th century was the successful solitary leader soliciting other skilled leaders to create a first-class worship service. The only option that will lead to missional success in the 21st century is an empowering leader activating effective teams, laser focused on the critical mission of the church—making disciples who make disciples.

Thus far, the shifts we've discussed have all had to do with the people of the church. But we are going to need to view buildings, land, and physical assets in a radical new way as well. That will be the topic of our next chapter.

IN THEIR OWN WORDS....

Franklin and Marisol Carrero served as the primary lead catalysts for the Rosedale Campus of Bethlehem Assembly, in the Rosedale neighborhood of Queens, New York. Here are lessons they learned in building a 21st-century team.

1. Please share a brief synopsis of your vocational and ministry experiences BEFORE you began the process of starting this new church. I came to the Bronx from the Dominican Republic when I was 17. I spoke very little English. When I came to this country, my mom worked at Fordham University for the custodial department. As

a result, I applied for and was accepted into a 12-month bilingual education program sponsored by Fordham University. During that year-long program, I needed to demonstrate an ability to write and communicate in English. I also needed to pass several core classes and demonstrate that I had the ability to enroll into a four-year program and have the skill set to succeed in college. As a result, I was one of 20 people that were accepted into a four-year program from 45 people that initially started the program at Fordham, and I was one of only four who successfully graduated from college from the whole group.

While attending Fordham, I started and managed several cell phone companies where I increased sales significantly year over year and managed to build a lot of relationships with people in the community. Upon graduation from Fordham, I was accepted into a program that gets one into the banking world. I decided to sell the cell phone businesses and transitioned into banking. My first job was as a branch manager taking care of personal clients and managing staff. Then I was promoted to a business banker and then VP and commercial banker managing well over $250MM in assets under management for many high-net worth business companies in the tri-state area, a business relations manager taking care of business clients. I have continued as a commercial banker to this day and continue to bring many large corporations to the bank I currently work for.

2. Give us a brief summary of the start-up process of your campus thus far.About eight years ago, my wife Marisol and I went through some medical and emotional challenges. On top of that we had a child

and were feeling pressured by the normal issues associated with parenting. We felt the need to pursue some things beyond financial security. A friend invited us to visit Bethlehem Assembly. The minute we walked into Bethlehem Assembly of God, we felt that God was calling us to give our lives to Jesus. In a matter of weeks, we surrendered our lives to Jesus. At first, we went through a pruning process. Then we began to sense the calling of God. Leadership confirmed it. We went to Bible School through the District School of Ministry. We began serving the local church very actively.

One of the first leadership roles we accepted was to mobilize teams to hand out flyers about the church. The project was very successful. Our pastor took note and invited us to get more involved. He introduced us to the idea of church planting. We went through an interview process and the interviewer discovered we had strong church-planting DNA. We began to pray about helping Bethlehem Assembly become a multi-site church. Pastor Steve Milazzo wanted the new campuses to have a neighborhood focus. We worked with him to develop a plan to start a campus through the process we learned through Urban Islands Project: creating awareness, building connections, forming relationships, and engaging in spiritual conversations. We recruited a missional team and for eight months we met, prayed, came up with specific strategies toward the community, and executed on that strategy. We prayed over the names the team had connected with. We continued building more momentum. Our launch team grew to 40 people. These were 40 people who considered themselves to be on a missions trip to their own community. We became aware of the needs of the community. God opened doors at the Rosedale schools. They allowed us and our team to come be part of some of their events. Then they asked us to run the events in the schools. We did outreaches, gardening, planting, movie nights, etc. Principals opened their doors and allowed us to invite people to do things with the church. After eight months, we held our first weekly service and our team of 40 celebrated as over 400 people from the neighborhood gathered to worship Jesus.

For 11 months following our first public gathering, every week (except one) we had at least a new person who came from the community. During COVID-19, we have remained faithful to the same schools. We've gathered groceries, hygiene products, etc. We've given out hundreds of care boxes to people from the Rosedale community. Even though COVID put a hold on the gathering, our team has remained faithful to what God has called us to do in the community.

I've learned four things through this process 1.) God prepares us in our past for the season of plowing, raking, and harvesting. 2.) I have the ability to inspire a group of people to be missional and go outside the four walls of the establishment. They will never be the same. 3.) The importance of keeping everything centered on Jesus. Jesus has been seen throughout this whole process. He has been represented in a very compassionate way. 4.) The Lord has been faithful to send people to us so we can disciple them.

3. What has been the most important lesson you've learned about building great teams? Having a clear mission and the vision made it easy for us as a church to put together a winning team. A clear

mission and vision enabled us to ask the right questions. We knew what we were looking for. We were not looking for shouters, we were looking for rakers. People that were willing to do the farming. Even if they were super-gifted, they were willing to wash others' feet. Raking is the method that builds the church. That's the way Jesus built it. When I see the disciples, they were generally uneducated. Many churches look for the education, pedigree, titles. Jesus was looking for hearts that were willing to plow. Yes, we need the gifts, but gifts don't build a church.

Having clear metrics has been very important because it allowed some people to remove themselves from the team because they were unwilling to be held accountable to the metrics. We were calling them to a place they'd never been before.

4. Anything else you'd like to share? Because I have a great energized team, I am able to continue to be a full-time banker while pastoring this campus. My ability to be successful as a banker has not suffered. The team allows me to do this. A lot of pastors think they need to quit their jobs to do this. If you really form a team who are willing to roll up their sleeves and work, you can do it.

SHIFT FIVE

REDEEM ARCHITECTURE

From empty buildings to fully utilized assets.

The team of seven Denver pioneer church starters started out doing what seems to come natural to every leader laying the foundation of a new church: looking for a place to gather for worship. They quickly found out that in densely populated urban neighborhoods, acquiring meeting space is easier said than done. If a space is available, the cost is often prohibitive or restrictions on the use make it unavailable to churches. Their collective frustration with the challenge came to a head at one of our monthly cohort meetings. After a robust conversation in pursuit of a solution, one of the leaders piped up, "I think we're going to have to change the way we think about the relationship of the church to buildings." Indeed.

I once saw a church sign in front of a church building that said, "This is the building where the First Baptist Church meets." It's a popular thing to say, but much harder to actually do. Our actions speak louder than our slogans. If we are honest, the prevailing viewpoint of the collective

20th-century Church was that it's not a "real" church until it owns property and has its own worship space. Some church organizations even viewed the building as a testimony to the greatness of God or a tangible reminder of God's presence. Ironically, many of these "churches" sat empty the vast majority of the time. The most active had things happening on Sundays and maybe a couple of times mid-week. But otherwise the buildings waited for people to occasionally show up.

The 20th-century view of architecture was mono. The 21st-century view is retina display. *Mono* refers to one use and one kind of location. For years, church growth experts were dispensing wisdom that went something like this… "To grow a successful church, you need at least five acres of land and adequate parking for the maximum capacity of your sanctuary." That advice served a lot of 20th-century churches well. They claimed their territory and claimed sacred space for a monochromatic purpose—church buildings were for worship services, Christian education classes, etc. The buildings were supported by tithes and offerings, and the main beneficiaries of the buildings were the tithe-paying members and the occasional non-member guests who darkened the doorway of the church building. The COVID-19 crisis of 2020 temporarily forced many churches to loosen their grip on the centrality of the building to the identity of the church, but the tendency to view church as a gathering in a building instead of a people on a mission remained intact.

For the Church to thrive, the monochromatic norms of the 20th century must give way to the retina display of the 21st century. Retina display on a phone is made up of millions of colors displayed by so many pixels that they are too small to be distinguished by the human eye. For the Church, *retina display* means the Church has left the building and can be found anywhere and everywhere. The gathered Church is popping up in all kinds of unexpected places. Coffee shops, dance studios, Section 8 Housing Recreation Rooms, houses, grade school cafeterias, and so on.

But perhaps even more revolutionary, the "sent" Church is showing up in unexpected places as well. The gathered Church is all about the "saving" side of discipleship. The sent Church is all about the "seeking" side of discipleship. When the Church is operating in full retina display mode, the sent Church will be showing up in company boardrooms, Little League games, office Christmas parties, school classrooms, civic clubs, homeowners association meetings, etc. In the monochrome days of the Church, real cChurch happened in a specific building dedicated for the purpose of gathering the Church. In the retina display days of the Church, the real Church is happening every place that people dedicated to being on mission with Jesus go.

Redeeming architecture means we release the Church from being confined to a solitary sacred space and recognize that wherever the people of the Church are, that space becomes a place where the Church is being manifested.

Am I saying that the 21st-century church will no longer own property or buildings? No way! But buildings and property of the 21st-century church will serve the mission of the Church, not the other way around. For example, buildings owned by the Church (the people of the church) will rarely be allowed to sit empty for long periods of time. "Yeah, but how?" you ask.

THEY WILL BE USED TO GENERATE INCOME.

21st-century church buildings will be used to generate revenue. Ministry funds should not be used to pay for buildings. Buildings should at least pay for themselves, and ideally, they should generate positive revenue to support the mission of the Church.

Some examples of buildings that pay for themselves could be buildings shared between a coffee shop and a church. The coffee shop pays for the meeting space and creates a great gathering place for people during the week that naturally lends itself to the building of redemptive relationships. Tithes and offering income is used to cover other ministry expenses. Corner Coffee Church in Minneapolis has numerous campuses that consist of a coffee shop six days a week and a worship space on Sundays.[16] Building costs are covered by the coffee shop profits. The gathered Church covers the other ministry expenses.

THEY WILL BE SHARED WITH THE COMMUNITY.

Perhaps even more exciting are the possibilities for the church actually becoming a catalyst for community transformation. An emerging trend in many places is flexible work and retail space that is used by multiple entities just during the time they need it. For example, a fitness studio that serves early bird fitness fans just needs a space from 4 a.m. to 10 a.m. every day. That same space could be used as a photography studio in the afternoon and host a church neighborhood Bible study at night. What if the church helped make such a shared-use partnership happen?

If we are willing to see the building as a tool to serve the mission of God, the possibilities are endless. Pop-up stores, community meetings, co-working space, church-sponsored personality profile discovery groups could all share the same space at different times. Sharing the cost of the space lowers the cost for everyone and places the church in close proximity to people who may never deliberately choose to visit a conventional

---

16   http://www.corner.coffee

church. An episode of The Future of Cities podcast entitled "Stoa" has some inspiring thoughts along these lines.17

THE CONCEPT OF CHURCH ARCHITECTURE WILL NOT BE LIMITED TO OWNED OR LEASED MEETING SPACE.

Redeeming architecture goes beyond multi-use of church buildings and properties. The 21st-century church views the spaces controlled by its members as part of the architecture of the church. Instead of defaulting to "building an education wing" as a solution for a place to do Christian education, 21st-century churches ask what spaces we already have access to that can be used for Christian education (and other purposes). Homes can become places the gathered church meets. Recreation centers, libraries, community centers where church members have influence can be potential space resources for housing ministry events and gatherings.

CHURCH ARCHITECTURE WILL INCLUDE SPACES OWNED BY OTHERS.

But it doesn't stop there. What about partnership with other non-profit organizations with a good reputation that are already serving in the community? In some cases, it might be best to use a gym owned by a Boys and Girls Club as a place to do your recreational league. I've heard of communities with three gyms that are empty most nights of the week and a church raising funds to build another gym for the glory of God. What if the church partnered with the community instead of building their own recreation space?

CHURCH BUILDINGS WILL BE UTILIZED FOR COMMUNITY TRANSFORMATION.

At the other end of the spectrum is the concept of a church building space as a way to serve the community. If an asset audit of a community

17   https://medium.com/sidewalk-talk/
city-of-the-future-podcast-episode-7-stoa-retail-69885f4a410f

reveals that three gyms have a waiting list of others who want access to a gym, a church might consider building a gym as a way of filling a gap in the community. I heard about a church in a small western town that realized the community lacked a really good park where people could gather for community recreation and events. The church received a donation of 120 acres from the disbursement of an inheritance. They decided to develop a park on much of the land to be used by the community. Their generosity was the talk of the town for years and a tangible benefit that raised the quality of life for everyone. Without saying a word, the Good News of the Gospel gained ground the day the park opened in that little town.

We get a little hint of how this attitude toward church architecture was the norm in the 1st-century church in the simple statement in Acts 2:46, "So continuing daily with one accord in the temple, and breaking bread from house to house, they ate their food with gladness and simplicity of heart..."[18] The early church clearly did not "own" the temple courts. They used them because they were available and accessible to the early Christian believers. They also shared the Lord's Supper together in the different homes of the earliest disciples. The following verse makes it clear that "the Lord added to their number daily those who were being saved." Lack of a building did not inhibit the forward motion of the earliest church because it was born with a retina display understanding of Church architecture. That vigorous expression of the Church expanded more rapidly than any building campaign process could accommodate.

A redeemed understanding of architecture will be crucial for the church to flourish in the 21st century. However, we should keep in mind that exploring these creative ideas without the benefit of business or non-profit

18   Acts 2:46 NKJV

sector experience will be perilous for leaders whose only training has been theological. Redeeming architecture creates a wonderful opportunity to involve experienced marketplace leaders in the conversation. The 20th-century church tended to view business leaders as pockets full of money. The 21st-century church will view them as colleagues full of wisdom and ideas that have the potential to exponentially increase the relevance of the local church and positively impact the neighborhood in ways that have never been seen before.

The 20th-century idea of a building with one purpose that is empty most of the time needs to give way to multi-use, multi-locational, frequently occupied, efficiently utilized spaces that incarnate the Church into every nook and cranny of the community.

Speaking of community...the 21st-century church must move on from the isolated communities of the 20th century to the complementary communities of the 21st. That will be the subject of our next chapter.

IN THEIR OWN WORDS...

Chad and Annette Smith are the founding leaders of Dwell Life, an emerging faith community in the Platt Park neighborhood of Denver. This is their story.

"Prior to planting the Dwell Life community, Annette and I were associate pastors for more than 15 years in New Jersey. Both of us, as pastor's kids, grew up in and around ministry of various sizes and styles; from rural to urban/suburban, from small, local church ministry to regional church oversight. As we began serving in ministry full-time, the unifying thread among the churches and ministries we served was that service time was King. Sunday services, Wednesday family night, student ministries, and all other activity needed dedicated space and time that, over time, actually served to erode our connection to the very community we hoped to serve. An unintended consequence of well-meaning plans was that the buildings became sacred, the methods became doctrinal, and the people (community) unassociated with the church and its activities became merely an afterthought. In many of these ways, our early ministry followed a well-worn path of activity lifted from the pages of expectation: minister to those already within the walls and pray for others to find sanctuary within the same walls.

"As we have developed Dwell Life here in Denver, this mindset has shifted. We began with a bold question: Is it possible for us to build relationships that will demand the church instead of building a church that demands relationships? Asking this question has required three key shifts: first, that we see the location of our home as sacred (God has placed us here to reach people that He is in desperate pursuit of); second, that we develop deep relationships with the people we live in closest proximity to and see this as doctrinal (it is the method God has given to accomplish the Gospel); and third, that we see the buildings and activities typically associated with "church" as the afterthought (they are the loosely held 'how' instead of the tightly guarded 'what.'

"Within the first year of living in our new, too-small, too-expensive, rented home in Denver, we shared a meal with more than 115 of our neighbors, nearly every person on our block and scores of others from the blocks nearby. Structured Bible studies began to form out of the friendships we held, even if the individuals were far from God or simply curious about Jesus. Eventually these in-home meetings began to function more like what we had previously known as 'Church services,' but our hearts and mindsets were vastly different. Our new motto became "Church Monday through Saturday, party on Sunday"…meaning the community involvement, conversations, and engagement in the homes of our neighbors during the week ARE the church, and Sunday is simply when we gather to celebrate what God has done in His church (the Party!).

"After years of paying too-high rent and living in too-cramped quarters for our family of five in our 1927 bungalow, an unexpected blessing came from this momentous shift in mindset. 'Dave and Laura,' friends who lived directly across the alley from us, had three children the same ages as ours and shared our Christian faith. Theirs was the "big house" on the block, newly built two ago. We had spent these last two years sharing meals, sharing game nights and movie nights, and sharing dreams of a neighborhood that looked like Jesus. And now they needed to move to London for work. They offered us the rental of their more-than-double-the-size home for literally half of what we had paid previously. The day our friends made their official move to London, we drove them to the airport to say goodbye. As we hugged one last time, Dave said, 'I'm so glad Dwell Life has a *place* befitting the *ministry*.' It finally rang true that the PLACE God had planted us was sacred for His purposes, the RELATIONSHIPS were doctrinal in how God wanted to share the Gospel, and now, we had a *place* befitting the *ministry* that God was already doing.

"Ultimately the goal for Dwell Life is to be what we call an Urban Barn, here in our neighborhood. In the traditional, rural sense, the barn is a place where the flock is cared for and safe. It's a place where the resources of the community are stored and dispersed as needed. And often, it's a place where the community folks gather for business deals, political discussion, and a good barn dance. Are there better ways to describe the mission of the church? Dwell Life should be a place where the community "flock" is cared for, nourished and safe; where kids have music lessons, STEM classes, and a safe early-learning environment; where resources like a food bank or a coat drive are stored and dispersed; a place where discussions of faith, business, and life happen intentionally and frequently...and maybe even where we have an occasional barn dance."

SHIFT SIX

RECLAIM THE ECOSYSTEM

From isolating to complementing.

The Denver Seven had an advantage right from the start. They had each other. Because they intentionally chose to take their start-up journey in the context of a cohort of peers, they did not face one of the most pervasive church start-up challenges: isolation. Most church starters, especially urban and rural, are "one of a kind" for their sending organization in their particular geography. This results in the probability that numerous church starters are unaware they are living and starting within just a few miles of each other. Even worse, their tendency toward church start-up tunnel vision might cause them to disregard the incredible ecosystem all around them. Sort of like what is happening in Australia.

Australia has a problem. First, it was believed they had too many dingoes. Dingoes are an "apex" predator, meaning they have few natural enemies. Permission was granted to hunt dingoes. As the dingo population declined, the kangaroo population soared to the point that Australia has twice as many "Roos" as people. They seem to be everywhere. The result is a complicated relationship with kangaroos. On the one hand, they are the most commonly known animal associated with Australia—a sort of natural national mascot. On the other hand, their numbers have reached what some are calling "plague proportions." The dingo/kangaroo debacle in Australia is a classic example of what happens when an ecosystem is not factored into strategic planning processes.19

Problems with the ecosystem begin when the existence of the ecosystem is disregarded. Well-intended people tamper with the ecosystem for reasons they deem appropriate—food, safety, sanitation, etc. The initial problem may be solved, but the repercussions that ripple through the ecosystem create other, perhaps more significant, problems and/or losses.

For the most part, the 20th-century Church functioned as if the ecclesiastical ecosystem did not exist. It was every church or church organization for itself. The result was thousands of Christian church organizations operating mostly in isolation from each other and at a missional level that was less than optimal.

For the Church to thrive in the 21st century, we are going to need to reclaim the ecosystem. Reclaiming the ecosystem begins with acknowledging there is an ecosystem that needs to be reclaimed. Otherwise, we will be content to go on our merry way unaware of the self-inflicted damage we are doing to the forward motion of the Mission of Jesus. In fact, in the same way that disrupting the natural ecosystem is an existential threat to life on Planet Earth, disregarding the ecclesiastical ecosystem will severely hamper our ability to serve God's purposes on this earth. Organizations

---

19   https://www.nationalgeographic.com/magazine/2019/02/
australia-kangaroo-beloved-symbol-becomes-pest/

that choose to go it alone will not only hurt themselves, but they will negatively impact the overall effectiveness of the Church that Jesus is building. We need to get this right!

AN OVERVIEW OF THE ECCLESIASTICAL ECOSYSTEM.

Obviously, metaphors have their limits. There are no apex predators in the ecclesiastical ecosystem. At least there should not be. The ecclesiastical ecosystem is made up of all the various people, churches, church organizations, etc. that are part of God's plan to carry out the Mission of Jesus on Planet Earth. Here is a partial list of some of the "organisms" that make up the ecclesiastical ecosystem.

Individual believers: Every person who is following Jesus is a part of the ecclesiastical ecosystem. This is both a blessing and a challenge. The blessing is that the vast diversity of people who are following Jesus is an amazing array of God's handiwork. According to the Pew Research Group, Christians are the largest religious group on earth, accounting for approximately 31 percent of the population of the planet, or about 2.3 billion people.[20] Islam is the next-largest religious group in the world with about 24 percent identifying with the Muslim faith. It's worth noting that Islam is currently the fastest-growing religion globally. In fact, according to Pew, by 2060, the general world population count is expected to increase by 32 percent, but the number of Muslims will increase by 70 percent over their current number (1.8 billion) while the number of Christians is projected to increase by about 34 percent. With all this in mind, it is crucial that we work together to optimize the missional effectiveness of every person who calls on the Name of the Lord.

---

20   https://www.pewresearch.org/fact-tank/2017/04/05/
christians-remain-worlds-largest-religious-group-but-they-are-declining-in-europe/

The local church. Localized expressions of the Body of Christ are the most visible manifestations of the presence of the Church that Jesus is building. Every local church is an invaluable part of the ecclesiastical ecosystem.

Denominational organizational structures. Despite the rapid emergence of non-denominational churches, most churches are still affiliated with a denomination. Typically, denominations have local, regional, and national representatives who seek to optimize the benefits of affiliation for local churches and newly emerging churches.

Church-starting networks. Toward the beginning of the 21st century, a new asset began to show up in the ecclesiastical ecosystem—church-starting networks. These networks transcend denominational boundaries and can serve as complementary agencies for denominational church-starting efforts. They can also provide a "home" for non-denominational church planters. Some examples of national church planting networks would be the Association of Related Churches (ARC) and Acts 29. Church-starting networks can also function inside the friendly confines of a denominational family. Some examples would be the Kairos Network that serves churches affiliated with the Lutheran Church: Missouri Synod and the Church Multiplication Network that serves churches affiliated with the Assemblies of God.

Church-starting support organizations. These are organizations that provide resources, services, and platforms for collaboration for anyone anywhere who is starting a new church. These church-starting support organizations typically work across denominational lines. Unlike church-starting networks, these organizations do not provide any oversight or formal accountable leadership structures. Urban Islands Project and Redeemer City to City would be examples of church-starting support organizations.

City movement organizations. Many cities now have interdenominational entities emerging that exist to help the ecosystem become self-aware and benefit from the rich ecclesiastical diversity that God has raised up to bless and redeem the city. A great example is The New York City Leadership Center founded by Mac Peer.[21] Over the years, Mac has patiently built connecting bridges between church organizations that have paved the way for powerful cooperative efforts empowering churches to accomplish more together than they could by themselves. It is important to note that the center grew out of a cooperative prayer effort called "Concerts of Prayer."

The general culture. General culture is like the ocean we are all swimming in. It is big and affects us in ways we are often unconscious of. For example, I once led a church start-up training event in the nation of Romania. The participants were seated around tables, and for purposes of group exercises, each table was a team. We introduced a team-building exercise by asking each team to lie on the floor in a circle with their feet in the air so that their feet formed a sort of platform. We then placed a bucket of water on the platform of feet and told the participants that they had to work together to remove their shoes without getting wet. My experience in doing this exercise had only been in the United States, so what happened next was a complete surprise and a great illustration of the power of culture. With all the teams ready to go, we challenged them to be the first team to remove their shoes without getting wet. We

---

21   https://movement.org

then yelled enthusiastically, "On your mark, get set..." but we never made it to "Go" because loud sounds of protest swelled up from all over the room. Our translator let us in on the problem. "They want to all watch each team do the exercise so they can cheer them on." Honestly, I was stunned. We were in fact doing a team-building exercise, and in the general American culture, winning is what matters the most. But in a nation with the remnants of a communist culture deeply baked into their collective perspective, helping each other be successful was what mattered most. Up to that point, I was unaware of how much the general American culture impacted how I thought about everything. My point is that the general culture impacts us all and it impacts the Church for good and unfortunately sometimes for not-so-good. The general culture is a real factor in the ecclesiastical ecosystem in which you dwell.

Local culture. Local culture is like a lagoon or beach in the ocean we all swim in. It is the collective personality of the town, suburb, or neighborhood where your church serves. Local culture is definitely influenced by the general culture, but it has distinctives that set it apart and give it its own unique cultural flavor. For example, the neighborhood I live in is composed of a lot of high-rise apartments and condo buildings. Parking is hard to find and expensive. The Central Business District of our city is just a short walk for everyone who lives in my neighborhood. Many residents in our neighborhood don't own a car, not because they can't afford one, but because it just doesn't make sense for them. They can choose a variety of other convenient ways to get where they want to go. My adult children and their families both live in suburban communities where one car is an absolute must and most households have at least two cars.

Walkable neighborhoods and car-based suburbs have very different local cultures. The sidewalks in my city neighborhood are constantly used by people on their way to do something. The sidewalks where my children live are used occasionally. I meet my neighbors in the elevator. They meet their neighbors across the backyard fence. I usually walk when I go out for a meal. They always drive if they want to eat in a restaurant. Local culture is a very important part of the ecclesiastical ecosystem because the shape of the local church will need to be appropriately informed by the local culture.

Civic government. Another impactful part of the ecclesiastical ecosystem is the government. Local governments typically have the most immediate impact on the well-being of the local church. Local interpretations of the concept of separation of church and state differ drastically from place to place. In one neighborhood, the local government might restrict the number of cars that can be parked on a street and in doing so inhibit the ability of a person to have a Bible study in their home. In other communities, the church may find itself in a privileged position because of the favor of local elected officials.

The list above is not exhaustive. Your particular context may have other elements that all add up to an amazing ecosystem for you to benefit from. Too often, churches view everything outside of their immediate organization as a threat to be avoided or a competitor to be overcome. Leaders of the 21st-century church will view the diverse elements of their ecosystem as resources to be tapped. Optimizing the benefits of your ecosystem is how your ecosystem will be redeemed.

HOW TO REDEEM THE ECOSYSTEM.

1. Do an ecosystem audit. List all the elements of the ecosystem surrounding you and your church.

2. Evaluate the relationship of your church to the surrounding ecosystem. Unaware, suspicious, somewhat engaged, fully utilizing the ecosystem.

3. Based on your analysis of each element, formulate action steps that will help you and those around you benefit from the ecosystem.

4. Discover your options for acting in complementary ways toward the rest of the ecosystem.

5. Factor the reality of the ecosystem into every decision your organization makes about how you interact with the general and local culture.

6. Repent of prideful isolation and commit to intentional actions that increase the Name and Fame of Jesus in the context of the community you serve.

I realize this chapter on redeeming the ecosystem may seem unnecessary to many who are reading this book. After all, every healthy ministry leader is aware of the multitude of scriptural admonitions toward unity. Clearly, God wants His Church to get along. We all say yes to "unity" as a matter of philosophy. But too often, our orthopraxy is out of alignment with our orthodoxy. It's not so much that we publicly disagree or compete with each other. Our disunity is usually displayed much more subtly. In fact, most often the ecosystem is underutilized because we simply act as if the other churches aren't there. We just stay away from each other and profess our unity from afar. It's way easier that way. You do your thing. We'll do our thing. And we'll pray for each other.

The truth is, working together is really hard to do. My observation is that many attempts to recognize the ecosystem are sabotaged right out of the gate for a variety of reasons. Sometimes the reasons are theological. But most of the time, the reasons have more to do with good old-fashioned personal preferences and organizational values. And sometimes, the reason is that we are using the wrong word to describe how we will actually work together.

That word is "collaborate." On the surface, it sounds like the word we want to use. The definition of "collaborate" is "to work, one with another; cooperate, as on a literary work."[22] That sounds exactly like what we want to do. But here's why, more often than not, attempts to collaborate end up with different organizations going their own separate ways and deliberately choosing not working together. True collaboration requires compromise. When two quality organizations decide to work with one another, inevitably there are going to be organizational values, habits, or characteristics that don't fit together well. In order to collaborate well, one or both of these organizations will need to compromise something that is important to them so that the two organizations can work well together.

But "compromise" is a bad word in the church world. One of the reasons great organizations become great is that they refuse to compromise, even on the little things. This is why attempts to truly collaborate often end in frustration and failure. Ironically, in order for us to walk in authentic unity and optimize the value and benefit of the entire ecosystem, we need to stop trying to collaborate!

This collaboration challenge is not limited to the confines of the church part of the ecosystem. Collaboration can be a roadblock to working well with other parts of the ecosystem. The idea of collaborating with organizations that are based on a secular worldview is even more daunting. How

22   https://www.dictionary.com/browse/collaborate?s=t

can we work with groups whose fundamental philosophical positions are at odds with a biblical worldview? Should we even try? The level of compromise would likely be unacceptable. Our best efforts at collaboration will quickly be sabotaged. Clearly, collaboration is not the answer.

But, you may be wondering, if we stop collaborating, how can we benefit from the unique gifts, skills, and attributes that different organizations bring to the ecosystem? May I suggest that instead of trying to collaborate, we instead seek to "complement" one another. When we complement each other, we are basically saying, "You be awesome at what you are good at and we will be awesome at what we are good at and where those two activities come together, we will work together at the intersection of our gifts."

For example, Urban Islands Project is a complementary organization. We complement the efforts of church-starting and sending organizations that seek to begin new faith communities in urban and underserved neighborhoods. Our area of expertise is the specific challenges that church starters in urban communities face. We operate like scaffolding that is built around the start.up process of a new urban church. We do not ask the sending organization to change anything about their doctrine, philosophies, and identity. We simply provide their church starters with knowledge about effective start-up practices in the urban context. The sending organization wins because they do not have to spend years making rookie mistakes in starting urban churches and their church starters continue to be fully engaged members of their organization. The church starters win because they gain access to knowledge, information, and support that their sending organization cannot supply them. Urban Islands Project wins because we exist to increase the presence of the Church in the urban context.

As you think about reclaiming the ecosystem, a great place to start is to think about how to complement the efforts of the other members of your ecosystem. How can you be you and yet add value to what others are doing? How can they be faithful to who they are and yet add value to the ministry calling that God has called your organization to fulfill? Discovering how to complement each other's efforts is an important skill to learn in the quest to reclaim the ecosystem. Using the concept of complementing as a guide opens up the entire ecosystem to be utilized for the advancement of God's Kingdom, without compromising Kingdom values.

By the way, collaboration is not a wrong thing to do altogether. There are many situations where collaboration is an absolutely powerful tool for maximizing your impact and benefitting from the gifts of the whole. However, collaboration happens best between organizations that are aligned in mission, vision, and values. Intra-organizational collaboration is an essential practice of healthy organizations. Collaboration, done well, is a very good thing indeed!

BENEFITS OF RECLAIMING THE ECOSYSTEM.

1. We really are better together.
2. You will accomplish far more than you would in isolation.
3. Others will accomplish far more because they benefit from you making yourself intentionally available to the ecosystem.
4. The voice of the Church will have the opportunity to tangibly influence the local, and potentially the general, culture.
4. Learning to factor the ecosystem into your plans may slow down your progress at first, but in the end, it will most likely speed it up. We call this slowing down to speed up!

These first few chapters have suggested some shifts that may feel a little overwhelming right now. In fact, it's likely that you are beginning to realize that your idea of the timeline for strengthening or starting or church may need to be modified. Recalibrating the timeline is the topic of our next shift.

IN THEIR OWN WORDS....

Marshall and Wesley Gallagher have a track record of leveraging their ecosystem. They currently serve as the key leaders of Hope Community Church, Nashville, Tennessee. Here's a summary of their journey.

https://www.hopewestnashville.com

Give us a brief synopsis of your vocational and ministry experiences BEFORE you began the process of starting a new church.

I (Marshall) grew up in the South (which means I was familiar with the church) but was not a "church kid." So that meant I went to somewhere around 15-20 churches infrequently until high school. I came to faith through Young Life (a parachurch ministry) and the "seeking and saving" mission that a handful of college students took toward me and my friends in high school. I didn't really attend a church regularly until the end of college, which was in Auburn, Alabama, a typical southeastern university town. While I was there I went to a contemporary Methodist church (although I had no idea what that meant) and a traditional Baptist church and was a part of an RUF small group. The church I attended before seminary, where I gained much of my lay leading experience (leading discipleship small groups, teaching Bible studies, etc.) was modeled after "rethinking church," which was sort of an ecclesiological buffet of Anglicanism, Baptist, Presbyterianism, and Bible churches tossed together and blended up and called non-denominational. I went to Gordon-Conwell Theological Seminary, which was north of Boston (which had its ecosystem differences, especially with approaches of mission and kingdom). GCTS was distinctly multi-denominational, which meant I had professors and class-mates who were Anglicans, Presbyterians, Congregationalists, Lutherans, and Baptists, and met people who had the same high view of Scripture from every denominational root. I worked for a Converge church, but it had been an American Baptist church. I came to know some Acts29 pastors and by the end would have called myself a reformed baptist (with an intentional lack of capitalizing any of those terms). I always called myself a denomina-tional mutt, but really I was an ecclesiological orphan, without a home in a particular place, and had experienced so many ecosystems that the idea of hard lines of demarcation that categorized the church landscape I grew up around didn't seem valuable for kingdom ministry. This grew even as I went out to start a new church by being exposed to all the networks and forms and models to start new churches. My convictions didn't change, but certainly my value of differences in the ecosystem of the ecclesiological community continued to grow.

What did the start-up process of your church look like?

We left our church and spent a year in a church planting residency role in another church, doing odd jobs, learning all the things we did not know, and shedding a lot of the preconceived notions of what it looks like to start a new church. We gathered a launch team over several months, but the week before we were supposed to start officially meeting as a launch team, we were presented with an opportunity to merge/join/jump into another church in a similar area of town as we were looking. So by God's providence and much to our surprise, we stopped the plant and became members of Hope Community Church, which was a small church in a quickly growing urban area of Nashville. The church had about 30 members and a bi-vocational pastor but had not directed its focus toward reaching the local neighborhood. So while I became the lead pastor, we still needed to inject a multiplication culture into the church. It wasn't a revitalization, just a small church with a surprisingly young crowd who had all that you would want in a tight community and was very internationally minded when it came to church planting and missions, but less locally focused.

That's the energy we are trying to bring into the church and what sort of oozes out of both of us. We teamed up with Converge Mid-America, a relationship that started in seminary through a multi-denominational Baptist network some friends and I started. Converge primarily took the "sending organization role." Being baptistic in the South meant you had to play with big brother, the Southern Baptist Convention. My ecclesiological community of pastors was composed mostly of that denomination, especially at the local level. They had a great international missions presence (the IMB) and a seminary a few hours away with subsidized tuition. It was a no-brainer to join them as well. Urban Islands Project provided a cohort to walk alongside a few other planters, in Nashville, with a similar timeline as us, which was a specifically focused ecosystem. The best part about all of this is during the merge, none of these things presented deal-breakers because each had a role to play. We still maximized multiple organizations, formal and informal, to steward our resources best.

How did you navigate the shift described in this chapter?

Through all my experiences and faith journey, it seemed only natural to incorporate different ecosystems. In fact, I honestly wondered why this was unique. I would ask myself "why don't they just connect with _____?" or "why is this group so threatened by _____?" It never made sense.

Anything else you'd like to share?

It's easy to become a selfish mercenary and lose your heart while trying to collaborate. It's far easier to "play nice" and not really have a genuine relationship with shared goals for a local neighborhood with other pastors, churches, and organizations. You won't agree on plenty of things. Especially at the local level, you will bump into one another (both metaphorically and literally). You'll get bothered that another church starts a Bible study in a coffee shop on the same day and same time as you...what the heck?! But it is worth it. There is not a relationship that lacks tension or conflict of some sort, and if we are to consider others more important than ourselves, ecclesiological and secular ecosystems should be approached in the same attitude. I don't always get excited when I hear about a new planter coming to our neighborhood. I get annoyed when I hear people say "this area NEEDS a Gospel/thriving/evangelistic/biblical/etc. church." I get defensive, selfish, insecure...it happens to all of us, and we are busy! But if Jesus is the end goal, I've got to put that above my pride, my organization, my home-town, my restaurants, my block, and do the hard work (even with a busy schedule) of unifying for the good of the neighborhood and the mission of Christ. Talk is cheap, too. Do it or don't. There isn't a pastor on earth who will disagree with this idea...but very few actually do it, and while it's painful to see a lot of pastors you respect let tribalism eat them up, it's great when brothers and sisters walk in unity. I think a hard thing to admit is that you might need them and they might need you.

SHIFT SEVEN

RECALIBRATE THE TIMELINE

From launching to emerging.

The Denver Seven all started out with an expectation that they would spend a year preparing to "launch" public services. We even decided to try to launch on the same day. We thought it would be amazing to start seven churches in the same city on the same day. However, because we all knew we were in uncharted territory, we decided to make the "launch" date a soft target to allow us to learn together what our best timeline should be. Our missional metrics helped us gauge the progress that each team was making, and about three months before the scheduled launch date, four of the churches decided they were ready to launch and three decided they needed more time to build their relational network. We decided to change the label of our collective launch day from "Launch" to "Celebration." We suggested that everybody do something to gather people from their community of focus together on Celebration Sunday. Some of them "launched" on Celebration Day. Others organized service projects.

The Hills Church was one of the projects that decided to delay their "launch." Instead of launching, they invited people from the neighborhood to attend an information meeting. One of the reasons they decided to delay their "launch" was that our metric tools were indicating that their relational network was underdeveloped, and they would not launch with their desired level of momentum. When launch day arrived, Cherri and I frenetically darted from place to place trying to get a taste of each of the celebration gatherings. The four churches that chose to "launch" all started strong. The three that chose to delay were all able to get a sense of their level of connection to the people of their community of focus.

Sure enough, The Hills Church information meeting gathered together about 20 people. This was after a year of working really hard to build relationships in the neighborhood. I met with the leaders of The Hills Church to help them debrief and decide how to move forward. Honestly, I expected them to be discouraged due to the small number of attendees for their information meeting. Instead, they were energized because they had discovered they were on the right track and just needed more time to increase the breadth and the depth of their relational network. They spent another year doing just that and "launched" 12 months after their initial information meeting. Around 150 people showed up, and The Hills Church is thriving to this day!

How long should it take to start a new church? In the 20th century, it was normal to expect a church starter to move into a community and start holding regular weekly services within six to 12 months after their arrival. It was also normal for a new church to be totally self-sustaining from tithes and offerings alone within two to three years. Therefore, the timeline for starting a thriving 20th-century church looked something like this:

Year One: Say "yes" to God's call, receive approval and funding from your sending organization, and launch weekly services as soon as possible. The funding must be adequate to get you through the first two to three years of the start-up process.

Year Two: Seek to grow the tithes and offering base rapidly to ensure that the church is quickly moving toward sustainability through tithes and offerings alone.

Year Three: Become a church completely sustained by tithes and offerings alone.

This 20th-century model depended greatly on the presence of inactive, de-active, disappointed, or dissatisfied Christians living in the target community. These Christians already have some understanding of biblical stewardship, so when they are invited to a worship gathering of the new church, they are not surprised when the offering plate is passed.

The 21st-century culture emanating from our cities creates a completely different context for starting churches.

THE TIMELINE OF A 21ST-CENTURY CHURCH START-UP.

In the chapter on reimagining discipleship, we suggested that the 21st-century church will need to engage in broadband discipleship with intentionality that covers the full spectrum of the journey of faith in Christ. The assumption of the 20th-century church has been that there are people already in the community looking for a church to attend. Because this assumption is increasingly less true in the 21st century, it means that church starters and strengtheners will need to factor in time for building a relational network and engaging in evangelism into their anticipated timeline. In our work with multiple urban church start-up projects, we've identified four phases that must be factored into the timeline expectations for the 21st-century church starter and their sending/overseeing organization.

Before we discuss the four phases, it is important to consider this critical question: "When does a church start?" In the 20th century, the answer to that question was straightforward—a church begins on "Launch" day. When a 20th-century church starter was asked how old their church was, the answer would be oriented around their launch date. "Our church is two years old" meant that the church had been conducting weekly meetings for two years. This idea was heavily influenced by the most popular way of understanding church health: "How many attend your Sunday morning worship service and how much money do they put in the offering plate?" Prior to the commencement of public gatherings, people in the pews and pennies in the plate could not be measured. The pre-launch activities of the church were viewed as preliminary activities that led up the start of the "real" church. Therefore, it was common to conclude that the church "started" on the "launch" date.

The answer to the "when does a church start" question is different in the 21st century. Another crucial question will help us understand how it will be different. Question: "When does human life start?" People guided by a solid biblical worldview answer "at conception" without hesitation. In other words, people do not suddenly become people when they enter the world through the birth canal. A person is a person at the moment of conception. A tremendous amount of critically important development takes place WHILE the person is forming in the mother's womb. Put another way, a person "starts" at conception and everything that occurs after their "start" is part of the story of their life.

And so it is with a 21st-century church. The new church is first conceived in the mind of God. He calls a leader to be the catalyst for the new church. The moment the calling is clear and confirmed in the heart of the catalyst, the church begins to live. In the earliest phase of the church, it will be unseen. During the earliest phases of formation, critically important developments are taking place that will impact the health of the church throughout its course of existence. In the same way that doctors do everything they can to keep the baby in the womb for the full term of the pregnancy, so we should not be in a hurry to have a "birth" day for the new church. The church "starts" as soon as it's conceived. Everything that happens after the "start" is part of the story of the church.

Not only is it important for leaders of new churches to understand this, it is also a crucial truth for pastors of existing churches to know. When you embark on a plan to reformat an existing church, it is helpful to review the total history of the church, including how and why it was started in the first place. It is possible that some current realities (both positive and negative) of the existing church can be traced back to the origins of the church. Perhaps it was started as the result of an ugly church split or a leader with a rebellious spirit. Those earliest seeds will produce fruit throughout the life of the church and must be dealt with properly for the reformatting process to succeed.

In the 21st century, churches will be considered "real" from the point of conception. They won't need to wait until they "launch" to begin being the church. They will begin with the catalyst acting as a disciple-maker who makes disciples who make disciples. At some point the growing community of disciples making disciples may become visible in a manner that resembles a 20th-century "launch." But the emergence of new churches in the 21st century will occur in a variety of forms. House churches, missional communities, online fellowships, distributed teams, etc.... The possibilities of the form of communities of disciples will be as creative as the mind of God Himself.

Our work with numerous urban neighborhood-focused churches has led us to conclude that the emergence of healthy 21st-century churches, while diverse in form, will generally happen in the following four phases.

Phase 1: Discernment (one to two years, maybe even longer)

During the discernment phase, several important steps need to be taken to set up the church starter/strengthener for the highest probability of success. Jesus told his followers to "count the cost," and the discernment phase is where the cost is counted. Here are some elements of starting and strengthening that need to be considered.

Verify the calling. At the beginning of the discernment phase, they may not even realize they are called to start or strengthen a church. Instead, they may experience a growing awareness of a serious missional need that is beyond the scope of their current context. Eventually, this awareness of the need transitions to a new awareness that God is calling them to become directly involved in doing something about the need. Their awareness of the "need" is often accompanied by a strong sense that "somebody needs to do something," quickly followed by a realization that the "somebody" might be them. At this point, it is wise for leaders to engage in an assessment process to help determine if starting a new church or strengthening an existing one is something they are "wired" for. Most sending organizations have access to a variety of assessment tools that can be helpful to the potential church starters. Assessment tools that identify effective church strengtheners are harder to find, but many resources have been produced that will help leaders lead their church in the right direction.

Identify the community of focus. Identifying the community of focus is crucial because although every church is called to reach everybody, the fact is that every church is started or strengthened in the context of a unique cultural reality. The cultural context will greatly impact the "shape" of the emerging church. For example, if the majority of the people in the neighborhood speak only Spanish, the emerging church needs to be aware of that and allow their ministry strategies to be formed by the cultural realities. These culturally informed ministry strategies will make the church more effective at reaching some people and less effective at reaching others. The church that exclusively uses Spanish as its language of communication will have a difficult time reaching non-Spanish speakers. This is why it is important to identify the community of focus, because every other step in the start-up or strengthening process will be impacted by the culture of the community of focus.

Discovering the community of focus is more of an art than a science. Prayer is the foundation of the process and must permeate every step along the way. After all, we are partnering with the One Who Is Building His Church. It's extremely important for us to go where He is sending us. The most common indicator of clarity concerning the community of focus is when the leader finds it difficult to envision doing anything else but raising up a community of believers to serve the spiritual needs of the particular place to which they are called.

Determine the financial sustainability strategy. As discussed in the chapter on reinventing funding, the 21st-century church requires a creative approach to financial sustainability. The financial sustainability strategy must be planned with the specific community of focus in mind, because each community will have its own unique set of assets and challenges. The first priority of the financial sustainability strategy will be making sure the church starter and family will be able to reside in the community for a minimum of five years, sustained by a realistic custom-made plan that will adequately meet their cost-of-living needs. Then, a strategy should be discovered for sustaining the anticipated costs of doing ministry. The financial sustainability strategy should be based on a comprehensive five-year projection of income and expenses. The income projections should include revenue from the five revenue streams discussed in "Reinventing Funding."

For this plan to be helpful, extensive research will need to be conducted in the community of focus, especially in the categories of non-profit partnerships and for-profit partnerships. This will take time, but in the long run it will save years of financial uncertainty and stress.

Lay the foundation for team-building. This process is discussed at length in the chapter on team-building. Team-building is most helpful when knowledge of the community of focus is factored into the process. This will help the church starter ensure the team is a good fit for the context. It will also help the potential team members more meaningfully to evaluate their decision to participate. The best team members feel just as called to the place as the church starter. The weakest team members are those who are there just to support the church starter. Suffice it to say, team-building will take time.

Determine your transition strategy. How will you transition from what you are now doing and move toward the community of focus? Will this require physical relocation or just reallocation of how you budget your time? Who needs to be aware of your transition and how should they be made aware? What are the costs of the transition? How will those be funded? How will the transition affect your family and how can you proactively make the transition as healthy as possible for them? All these questions are important and need to be considered before you set the transition process in motion.

Affirmation of the call, clarity about the people/place, strong plan for financial sustainability, initial team-building efforts and a healthy transition strategy—these all take time and they all need to be done in advance of the second phase of the start-up process. A possible and even positive outcome of this phase is that the potential church starter or reformatter will realize, having counted the cost, that this is something they should NOT do.

Phase 2: Deploy (one to two years)

The church starter and team are confidently deployed into the community of focus, which is a fancy way of saying they move into the neighborhood. I love Eugene Peterson's rendering of John 1:14: "The Word became flesh and blood, and moved into the neighborhood..."[23] Moving into the neighborhood incarnates the presence of the Church that Jesus is building into that neighborhood. The presence of the people of the Church is the greatest need in a neighborhood where the presence of the Church is thin.

In the 20th-century model of church-starting, the deploy phase was three to six months. The goal was to get the word out quickly and make contact with people in the community who are looking for a new church experience. Three to six months was more than enough time. But the emerging

---

23   John 1:14 The Message

reality of the 21st-century culture means the deploy phase is going to take a lot longer because there simply aren't enough resident Christians to form the critical mass needed for a strong start process. Like the discover phase, the deploy phase has several actionable themes that require time.

Listen. The temptation of every church starter/reformatter is to move into the neighborhood and start shouting the news—we're here, God loves you, let's get together and worship Him. But the nature of the 21st-century culture requires that we be slow to speak and quick to hear. The first responsibility of the church start-up/reformat team is to understand the culture of the neighborhood. This understanding will come through listening. The key activity in the first three to six months will be listening to the residents of the neighborhood. What are they excited about? What are they afraid of? What do they do for recreation? What do they do for work? How do they define family? Etc.

Build relationships. In the chapter on discipleship, we discussed the importance of understanding relationships as the foundation of discipleship. Once the team has a sense of the key cultural distinctive of the neighborhood, it's time for them to intentionally build relationships with community residents. As we discussed earlier in the book, this takes time and it must be intentional. Questions that are helpful in this step include: What activities can I go to or invite others into that are great environments for relationship-building? For example, a loud environment (concert, etc.) is not a great place to hear about someone's life. But a quiet meal together is a great place to share life stories together. What are community projects I can get involved in that will lend themselves to relationship-forming/building? For example, volunteering to help build a trail or clean up a school will put you in proximity to others in a context where sharing life stories is natural.

Intentionally engage in disciple-making as described in the chapter on discipleship reimagined. Deliberately helping people move toward Jesus through positive awareness, personal prayer, redemptive relationship, and spiritual conversations will be your first priority during the deploy phase.

Identify the ideal form and rhythm for the emerging church. Now that you have a growing understanding of the ethos of the community, it's time to determine the optimal form and rhythm of the church. Should it be a coffee shop church, a house church network, a needs-based fellowship, a compassion bridge, a something else? How often should the worshipping community gather for worship, service, teaching, etc.? How does the church schedule need to be informed by the community? Is a building a necessity and if so, what type of building do we need?

The natural transition from the deploy phase to the next phase is when the church begins to hold regular weekly public worship gatherings. In the 20th century, this point in the process was commonly called "Launch," and "Launch Sunday" was a really big deal, because for many people it represented the point where the church actually starts.

In the 21st-century church, the start date of the church is when the church start-up leaders recognize God's calling on their life and say "Yes." From that point forward, the church has already started. It's very much like the process of a developing baby. The biblical understanding of life is that it begins at conception and everything from then on is a phase of life—including the birth day. In the same way, once the start-up catalyst says yes to God and joins with Jesus as He builds His Church, the church is already started. But like the birth day of a child, a new church will reach a point where it becomes publicly known and recognized as a church. In the same way, an existing church undergoing a reformatting process will likely experience a point where the new reality of the reformatted church emerges. When the church is publicly known, it moves into the develop phase.

Phase Three: Develop (one to two years)

It is during this phase that the basic "habits" of the worshipping community become fixed and effective. The formation of communal "habits" is the reason the local church exists. The alternative would be a completely laissez-faire approach where everyone just did their own thing and ministries and gatherings happened spontaneously. Lack of intentionality toward being the gathered and the sent church is not an option. The writer of Hebrews reminds us not to forego the assembling of ourselves together. We know the early church met daily in the Temple courts and from house to house. We are intended to journey together, and the newly formed or reformatted local church provides structure for that journey.

Develop missional rhythms. It is during the develop phase of the start-up process that the rhythms of the church become solid and appropriately informed by the rhythm of the greater culture. Depending on the rhythms of the neighborhood, the best time for the worshipping community to gather might be Sunday morning at 11 a.m. But in another neighborhood, the best time might be Friday night at 7 p.m. Other training, teaching, and ministry rhythms should be developed to maximize their benefit in that particular neighborhood.

Organize the organism. The develop phase will also include creating healthy financial habits, governance structures, and organizational systems and policies appropriate for the church style and cultural context. The organizational structures will vary based on church style and leadership preferences. The important thing is that they are clearly spelled out and that they support the mission. This is especially true for more organic forms of church that have less obvious structure. The less obvious the structure, the more important it will be for the leadership to clearly spell out how decisions will be made, money will be processed, etc.

Form healthy organizational habits. Organizational habits include answering the question how collective missional decisions will be made, money will be spent, leaders will be empowered, etc. These structures are important because they increase the probability of the long-term effectiveness of the worshipping community in that neighborhood. Once the church has become stable and established good organizational habits, they are ready to move to the next phase—duplication.

Phase Four: Duplication (one to two years)

The biblical template for the advancement of the Church is through multiplication. God told Adam and Eve to be fruitful and multiply. That's how the planet became home to 8 billion people and counting. He told His Church to go make disciples. That's His plan to fill the earth with His Church. A church without a plan to multiply is not participating in the normal life of the Kingdom.

Determine how you will duplicate. Some forms of being the Church are more easily multiplied than others. It's more difficult to reproduce a large, complex organizational church than it is to multiply a simple, more organic expression of the Church. The 21st-century church will trend toward being more organic and simple, which means multiplication will be more likely to become the norm rather than the exception.

Build duplication on a solid foundation. The foundation of duplication is leadership development. The foundation of leadership development is making disciples. The good news is that churches started through a process that is informed by the paradigm of reimagined discipleship will find it natural to develop leaders and send some of them out as catalysts for the next needed church in a different neighborhood.

Clearly, the timeline of a 21st-century church start-up will likely be significantly different than that of the prototypical 20th-century church start-up. It's not unusual for a 20th-century church to go from conception to fully functioning in three years or less. The start-up timeline for a 21st-century church will be at least four years and might take eight or even more. Church starters and church sending organizations will do well to align their expectations with this emerging reality.

The 21st-century timeline will be dramatically different than that of the 20th century. Another huge 21st-century change will be how we measure our missional progress. That will be the subject of our next chapter.

21st Century Timeline.

IN THEIR OWN WORDS....

Jarrad and Dawn Gibler are church starters on a journey of discovery. Their story is a perfect illustration of viewing starting a new faith community as a marathon, not a sprint.

Give us a brief synopsis of your vocational and ministry experiences BEFORE you began the process of starting this new church.

Ever since I (Jarrad) became a Christian in my sophomore year of high school, I have spent my life in service to a local church. Most of those years were in a lay leader capacity in student and worship ministry, while I worked as a professional musician throughout most of my 20s. In 2009 I accepted a full-time position as the worship pastor of that same church.

Dawn was a public school teacher for several years before we met and were married. A year after I came on staff at our church, she was offered a full-time position as the student ministries pastor. We served together in student, worship, and inner-city ministry until we stepped down from our positions at the end of May 2018.

Describe the start-up process of your church thus far.

The start-up process for our church has actually been more of a restart process for our lives in general. Dawn and I have always been all-in kind of people, so every bit of our lives—our marriage, our children's schooling, our schedules—was geared around effectively and excellently fulfilling the ministry endeavors to which God had called us. Once we stepped away from those traditional ministry roles, the context upon which our social and family life was based radically shifted. And honestly, I wasn't prepared for it.

Our roles were very often physically and emotionally demanding, but they were also creative, dynamic, and flexible. We stepped away from leading ministries, casting vision, and implementing strategies; Dawn stepped back into public education (a role to which she had never wanted to return), and I ended up mopping floors at an elementary school (among other things). These past two years have been the hardest of our lives as we have been in the process of reworking how we join with Christ in His mission, while at the same time relearning how to spend time with our kids, pay our bills, connect with others, and even engage with each other as husband and wife.

However, in the midst of all the confusion and uncertainty, we still feel the call to live out our identity in Christ and be engaged with His purpose. Although we are not "where" we want to be, we are trying to give our best to what is right in front of us as we stay mindful of what is ahead of us. Currently, Dawn is mentoring a couple of emerging leaders, as well as helping with an anti-human trafficking ministry in inner-city Houston. I am meeting with a couple of young men as well and will start mentoring at a local junior high school this week. We will also be starting a small group in our apartment next week for our residents.

With the shift described in this chapter in mind, describe the process of your own journey.

I remember having a conversation with Dawn back in 2013, the theme of which centered on the Church's general need to rethink ministry, as well as our specific need to shift our own thinking and approach to better lead an emerging generation. Certain events from that year helped us look into our future and realize that we had to learn how to be the Body without the building, to give our students purpose independent of programs, and to call them to a clear and costly mission—one that answered the innate, God-given desire of their souls.

Although a lot of the process had been a journey into the unknown, a few overarching principles became strikingly clear:

1. Disciples making disciples is the foundational measure of success. We stopped worrying about how many students we had on a Wednesday night, and began to focus on how many students we were engaging with in one-on-one or small group discipleship throughout the week. Ultimately, the number that was most precious to us was the number of leaders we had empowered and released to start discipling on their own. These were more than a number, they were students with whom we had developed deep relationships...they had become family.

2. Discipleship truly is a family thing, and not a program thing. There is a vast difference between people who approve of Christ versus those who actually follow Him. Followers of Christ aren't produced, they are reproduced. And reproduction happens...well, in families.

People will never truly understand that which they do not live out. We began to focus less on concepts and sermons, and more on identity and missional living. We discovered that there was more growth—more relational and discipleship equity—in one week of teaching identity in Christ and leading students into actively engaging in ministry with us than there was in a year's worth of sermons. I love to teach, and I believe that sermons still have a place in the emerging Church. But the Apostle Paul was onto something when he said that the point of leadership was to empower the Body for the work of ministry...not the reception of it.

After rethinking our ministry and engaging with students from this mindset, we received one of the most profound compliments I have ever heard when a student, newly saved, said to us, "I had no idea that this is what Christianity was supposed to be like."

Anything else you'd like to share?

As we have been in this process of church planting for almost two years now, we have discovered that it is less a matter of an urban church that we are planting, and more a mindset of the future Church that we are helping to plant. Although Chicago was our focus when we initially took this leap of faith, at this point we are less worried about where we land, and more focused on how we are living in the process. So whether it's Houston today or Chicago tomorrow, we will make disciples.

SHIFT EIGHT

REFRESH THE METRICS

From bodies in the pews to disciples in the marketplace.

As they gathered for yet another cohort meeting, the general consensus of the Denver Seven was perplexity. It was "e-newsletter" time—the monthly touchpoint with faithful supporters to keep them up to date with the progress of the new churches. Every one of the leaders had just finished sharing amazing stories about how God was at work in their neighborhood. Deeply spiritual conversations with atheists. Walking with neighbors through job losses and relationship breakdowns. Connecting regularly with friends over coffee and meals. Praying with others about needs in their lives.

The anecdotal stories were amazing but not appropriate to share publicly. In many ways, every leader was more engaged in ministry to people than ever before. But so much of what was happening was internal, it was difficult to figure out how to share it in a tangible form that supporters would understand and be able to celebrate. Thus, their collective posture of perplexity.

"What gets measured gets done," says common sense. This simple idea has been around for centuries and is the basis for much of what goes on in the modern world. From the stock market to the boardroom and even to the church leadership team, keeping track of things determines where funding and energy will be directed.

In the church world, for at least a century, the gold standard has been noses and nickels. "How many you runnin'?" has become the key metric that quickly determines the pecking order in any room of church leaders. He or she with the most people (noses) in the pews on Sunday is automatically elevated in the eyes of his or her peers to the status of the best of the bunch. The other metric (nickels) is viewed as important, but asking about money is a little tricky in any circle. Savvy leaders have learned to toss out little hints like "Missions Giving" numbers that help others recognize the missional magnitude and financial health of the church at the same time.

Noses and nickels are the focus of most church growth training events. "How to gather more people and how to get the most money from those you gather" could easily be the most popular breakout session at a church growth conference. Why? Because we have become convinced that if these two numbers are increasing over time, that is the sign of a healthy, effective church.

The truth is that these numbers tell only part of the story. Too many unhealthy churches have a lot of people in the pews and plenty of money in the bank. But they are missionally sterile, stuck, or sick. They walk through the church calendar every year, dutifully celebrating key Christian holidays, hosting outreach events, and even graduating mature "disciples." But everyone knows something is off.

Relying on noses and nickels as the sole source of feedback regarding the health of a church is analogous to deciding if a car is operating properly by looking at the speedometer and the gas gauge. They do tell us something about how the car is performing. It is indeed possible that a car traveling 65 miles per hour with a full tank of gas might mean the car is operating properly. But it is also possible that the reason the car is traveling at 65 miles per hour is that it is hurtling downhill headed for a cliff with no engine and no brakes. If that is the case, the rate of travel and level of the gas in the tank would both be very bad news. That's why cars are equipped with other gauges and warning lights, including the dreaded "Check Engine" light. Typically, the better the car, the more comprehensive the performance feedback it provides the driver.

In the same way, thriving churches in the 21st century will be equipped with a comprehensive dashboard with other gauges and warning lights besides noses and nickels. Don't misunderstand what I'm saying. Noses and nickels do indeed tell us something about the health level of a church. But they don't tell us everything we need to know, and if we base our church health assessment on noses and nickels alone, it is very possible we will not have an accurate understanding of what is truly happening in the heart of the church.

The global COVID crisis exposed the weakness of our ecclesiastical love affair with noses and nickels. Noses became "ratings," "views," "comments," etc. Nickels became online donations, period. No more carefully crafted stewardship thoughts before the offering plates are passed. Many churches were completely disoriented with this detachment from their preferred scorecard. However, the churches that went on to thrive in the post-COVID world quickly discovered some new gauges and lights on the dashboard to help them assess their missional progress. It turns out that these new metrics discovered in crisis were very similar to the ones that had been discovered by urban church start-up pioneers we've worked with.

DISCOVERING THE 21ST-CENTURY MISSIONAL METRICS DASHBOARD

Earlier in this chapter we shared the quote of unknown origin that states "What gets measured gets done." To understand what we need to measure, we first need to think about what needs to get done. In an earlier chapter we were reminded that Jesus never told us to start churches. In fact, He never told us to build church buildings or church organizations. He did tell us that He is building His Church and He did give us the prime directive that we are to "go and make disciples." Jesus is building His Church on a platform of discipleship. Making disciples is something that needs to get done and should definitely be measured.

As we discussed in the chapter on reimagining discipleship, a challenge for the 21st-century church is that we have inherited a substandard definition of discipleship. Our inherited definition typically views discipleship as one of the ministries of the church or a program that every church needs to have, like boys or girls development programs. As a result, we typically measure discipleship in terms of how many people are going through our discipleship classes, attending our small groups or engaging in one-on-one discipleship relationships. These may be important metrics to add to our noses and nickels gauges. But they are still just barely scratching the surface. The scriptural definition of discipleship is far more holistic and comprehensive than our inherited one. The inherited definition tends to focus on the pos-salvation side of the discipleship journey. When we are guided by the scriptural definition of discipleship, we will include the pre-salvation actions of discipleship that can be measured.

If measuring noses and nickels is giving us only part of the information we need, what other gauges need to be added to our dashboard? With broadband disciple-making in mind, here are some gauges we should consider adding to our 21st-century missional dashboard.

Awareness Gauge: How many people are aware of you/the church in a positive way?

Connections Gauge: How many from the awareness category do you know by name, they know you know their name, and you are praying for them on a regular basis?

Relationships Gauge: How many from the connections category do you know their story, they know you know their story, and you connect with them on a regular basis?

Spiritual Conversations Gauge: How many from the relationships category know that you know Jesus and you want them to know and/or grow in Jesus?

Belong Gauge: How many from the spiritual conversations category gather together regularly for worship?

Believe Gauge: How many from the belong category have made a public profession of faith? (Perhaps this is the point of water baptism.)

Engage Gauge: How many from the believe category are engaged in the everyday life of the community of disciples?

Grow Gauge: How many from the engage category are intentionally seeking to mature in their walk with Jesus?

Minister Gauge: How many from the grow category have found a place of regular ministry and service in the community of disciples?

Multiply Gauge: How many from the minister category have become activated disciple makers by making people aware of them in a positive way, praying for people by name, cultivating redemptive relationships, enjoying spiritual conversations, inviting outsiders to belong, helping belongers believe, enabling believers to engage, encouraging the engagers to grow, challenging the growers to minister, and inspiring the ministers to multiply?

Consider the following two hypothetical examples that illustrate the contrast between being guided by 20th-century metrics and 21st-century ones.

Exhibit A: First Church is a 35-year-old church in their strategic planning process for the coming year of ministry. They use noses and nickels as their primary measurements of missional metrics. They are a church that gathers 300 for worship on a typical weekend. They have decided that they want to "grow" by 10 percent during the next calendar year. By "grow," they mean increase their Sunday morning attendance by 10 percent or 30 people. The first result of this goal is that it causes them to focus on the Sunday morning worship attendance as the key metric. The path to success is figuring out how to get more people to attend the morning worship services. Their strategy for increasing their worship attendance by 10 percent will include the usual suspects—a skillful advertising campaign, friend days, special sermon series, outstanding worship experiences, etc. Their advertising budget will be devoted to getting the word out about the quality of the worship experience. But there will be very little correlation between the things they do to attract people to their meetings and the results. Everything they do will be done in the hopes that the outcome will be more noses and more nickels.

Exhibit B: Second Church decides to set their goals based on 21st-century metrics that measure disciple-making progress. Second Church is also a church that gathers 300 to their weekend gatherings. They decide to ask God to help them increase their congregational number of disciples who make disciples by five new activated disciple makers. Based on their understanding of how disciples are made, they realize that for their efforts to "produce" 5 activated disciple makers, they will need to inspire 10 ministers toward becoming multipliers, challenge 20 growers to become ministers, assist 30 who are engaged to become intentional about growing, help 40 believers to become engaged, invite 60 belongers to believe, engage in spiritual conversations with 300 new people, form 900 new relationships, learn the names of and pray for 1,800 new friends, and make 18,000 new people aware of them in a positive way.[24] Instead of asking how to get people to attend worship services, the focus of Second Church is on being sent out to join Jesus on His mission. Their ministry strategies, church calendar events, ministry rhythm, etc. all will be built around engaging in broadband disciple-making activities. When they sponsor or participate in community events throughout the year, they will be paying attention to making progress in the different categories that represent missional advance. For example, they can participate in the local harvest festival by distributing complimentary hot chocolate and intentionally learning the names of as many of their neighbors as possible so they can pray for them. They will know that as they pray for people, they will be laying the groundwork for redemptive relationships to form that will lead to spiritual conversations that will lead to people choosing to follow Jesus and eventually become multiplying disciples.

---

24   See the "Open Hands" diagram.

OPEN HANDS

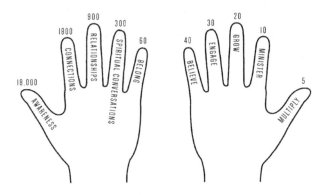

The ministry energy of Second Church will be focused primarily on making disciples, but their happy surprise will be that as a result of their efforts, an average of an additional 60 people will choose to join them every week for worship, meaning their noses number will go from 300 to 360 every week. But their focus will be on activating disciple makers instead of people in the pews.

Getting the metrics right is more than just a good idea. It will likely make the difference between good intentions and actual missional actions. Talking the talk without walking the walk has always been a challenge for the church. Metrics help talk become walk. Why? Because having agreed upon metrics helps us connect our orthodoxy to our orthopraxy.

For example, for a long time, I was frustrated by conversations with new church starters that went something like this:

Me: "How are you doing John?"

John: "Great! God is so good!"

Me: "Well, yes, that is true. What are you doing to make progress on starting the church?"

John: "We are building relationships with a lot of people."

Me: "Great! How many?"

John: "A lot."

Me: "What are the names of some of the people you are building relationships with?"

John: "Uh.... Jarrad and his wife... uh, I can't think of her name?"

Same conversation with solid, agreed-upon metrics.

Me: "Hey John, how's it going?"

John: "Great! In the last 30 days, we've made 400 new people aware of us in a positive way, connected with 75 new people, initiated 10 new relationships, and had significant spiritual conversations with three people who were previously disconnected from Christ and His Church."

Me: "So good to hear. How does the coming month look for you?"

John: We've planned some events that have the potential of connecting us with at least 100 new people over the next 30 days. We think we can initiate 25 new relationships through our neighborhood meet-up strategy. We're hoping to engage in spiritual conversations with seven new people. We also have 15 people signed up for our new Alpha Group. Our last Alpha Group had seven participants and five of them decided to follow Jesus and are being baptized next week."

Solid, missionally relevant metrics help everyone. Church starters are helped because they are able to report their progress in tangible ways. Sending organizations are helped because they have a more accurate picture of the progress being made by their sent church starters. Supporters are helped because they have a clearer understanding of the impact of their stewardship.

Some readers may be asking the question, where is the Holy Spirit in all of this? The answer—He's right in the middle of this story. Ministry is one part strategy and one part miracle. Someone else has said it's one part sweat and one part mystery. When we serve as co-laborers with Christ, our part is to bring the sweat and strategy and His part is to bring the miracles and mystery. Making disciples is how we co-labor with Jesus to build His Church. The intentional strategic steps described in this chapter represent our meaningful, purposeful actions that join with the supernatural work of the Spirit to move people toward faith in Christ. Effective 21st-century churches will no longer be guided by 20th-century metrics. They will align what they measure with what Jesus wants to get done—making disciples!

IN THEIR OWN WORDS....

Lisa and Eric Clements are the founders and key leaders of North Dallas Assembly in the North Dallas neighborhood of Dallas, Texas. Here's their 20th-to-21st-century transition story.

"Church planting required Eric and me to shift in so many ways. I had worked as an associate pastor for a large church in Kansas City for 13 years. What started out as a volunteer position in a church of about 250 turned into an executive leadership position of a church of 1,000 on Sunday mornings. I knew how to do big church and as a part of the executive team, I worked to make the transition at each level to a church of 1,000. This meant working with a large team of people. Together we built impactful programs that enabled people to grow closer to Jesus.

Moving to Dallas, I wondered how I would serve. Church-planting never even occurred to me. In fact, being a lead pastor was not something I considered. These two things, entrepreneurial planting and seeing myself as the senior leader, were the biggest mind shifts that occurred. Church planting was something I thought young guys who could not find a church did. I frankly did not see myself as a lead pastor. This was my own limiting belief. There are probably many reasons why I had that belief, and I was the only one who could change that. When our district asked me to consider being a lead pastor, I did not respond immediately. As I prayed, the Lord showed me that my own thoughts of myself were limiting what God wanted to do.

As I look back, I laugh. I approached church planting like I would a big project in a large church. I was used to fishing in a big, familiar pond. I knew where the deep waters (pockets) were. I knew who was gifted to do which jobs and what bait to use to get them on the team. In Dallas, however, I found myself at point zero. There were no people, no capital from relationships, and no deep pockets. Unfortunately, it took longer than I want to admit for me to change my mindset. I thought I knew how to do church. What I realized is I knew how to do church in a specific setting. I needed to lean into God to ask Him how to do church in my new neighborhood.

Neighborhood. Now that's a concept. Even though Eric and I lived in a neighborhood in Kansas for almost 14 years, I am not sure the neighbors miss us. Don't get me wrong, we were good neighbors. If being a good neighbor includes keeping your yard nice, waving as you drive by, and loaning the occasional cup of sugar. That kind of neighbor is easily replaced. We did not know our neighbors because we were always at church. All our ministry took place at church. I found my friend life, work life, and spiritual life were enmeshed in this one building. We didn't spend much time with our neighbors in our neighborhood. Foolishly, I was afraid to ask them to my house because they might bring alcohol. Then what would people think? I know, I know, this is crazy-thinking. That's where we found ourselves. We were more concerned about looking like good Christians, serving the Lord all the time, and pouring our life blood into church. Our motives were good. We wanted desperately to serve God, and we were. However, we limited our reach. We defined our "ministry" by what took place inside the church. Our goal was to get people to church. This is not a bad thing, but it is a small thing.

We began to rethink our neighborhood. We invited our actual neighbors to a BBQ in our backyard. We didn't talk about church, we listened to hear their stories. It was great fun. Who knew our new neighbor was Ronald McDonald! Yes, the real guy. He worked for McDonald's for 25 years. He is also a professional magician. Another neighbor has lived in our neighborhood since 1963. She knows the area, the changes, the history. We did this over and over again. Eric and I began to view our neighbors as people who bear the image of God. I hate to admit it, but before I had seen people as projects.

We did have a big project. We were starting a church. Shifting our mindset from people are projects to people are image bearers changed everything. We had only begun to grasp what this meant to the church planting endeavor when we joined an Urban Islands Project Cohort. They helped us bridge the gap from our previous church mindset to our current mindset.

I began to see myself as our neighborhood pastor. We looked for ways to truly be neighbors. We were not looking for a way to get people to church. As we began to learn people's names, to pray for them, and look for ways to hear their stories, people began coming to church. I would love to say everyone came, but they did not. It did, however, open doors for ministry. I have prayed with the sick, counseled marriage crisis, prayed on front porches, grieved over a stillborn child and a deceased spouse. As my mindset opened to the possibility of being the church, amazing opportunities to share Christ occurred.

That brings me to COVID-19, another shift in our ministry. At the time of this writing, we are still meeting online exclusively. The Lord is at work. Being online has provided a non-threatening way for some of my neighbors to peek in and see us. Even though we have live streamed from the beginning, they seem more open to logging in now. One neighbor commented she watched my "talk" online. "I really liked it. I am going to watch again." I am not sure what will become of this relationship later. I do know that God is at work. Every day that I let go of how I "think" it should be done, I see Him expand my territory and my vision.

SHIFT NINE
REFOCUS CHURCH HABITS
From calendar-driven to mission-driven.

Every one of the leaders of the Denver Seven churches were formed and shaped by the 20th century church. Intuitively they knew that much of what had shaped them would not apply in the urban context, and that the churches they were starting would not look like the churches they grew up in. Yet, the gravitational pull of their 20th-century habits was tough to overcome.

As they met monthly to wrestle with how a 21st-century church will look, it began to dawn on them that their 20th-century habits orbited around the "saving" side of the mission of Jesus—helping the already-convinced become surer of and stronger in their faith. Their efforts to start new churches in neighborhoods with very few Christians had pushed them to focus their time and energy on the "seeking" side of the mission of Jesus. They were concerned that when they added in the "saving" side activities, the "seeking" side would get lost in the shuffle. They collectively realized that the habits of the 21st-century church would need to be very different from her 20th-century counterpart. Cautiously, they began to experiment with potential 21st-century habits. Here's what they learned.

Their collective reflections on their 20th-century church journey resembled my own. The 20th-century church I grew up in was very intentional about being the gathered church. My family was every 20th-century pastor's dream family. We were a model of involvement in the life of the church. Our week started off when the bell rang announcing it was time for Sunday School at 9:45 a.m. on Sunday. After a brief break, it was time for the Sunday morning service at 11 a.m. Around 12:30 p.m., the benediction was prayed and after several brief conversations in the hallway and the parking lot, our family headed home for Sunday family dinner. Quite often, the menu consisted of roast beef (slow-cooked while we were at church, filling the house with an unforgettably pleasant aroma) mashed potatoes, green beans, and some yeast rolls. After Sunday dinner, our bellies full of wonderful food, it was time for our Sunday nap. After catching a few lazy Zs, it was time for me to head to church for some sort of practice—choir, Bible quiz, drama, etc. The practice would last right up to the commencement of the Sunday Evening Evangelistic Service at 7 p.m. I never did fully understand why it was called that, because we did basically the same thing on Sunday night that we did on Sunday morning, except on Sunday night the service always ended with time at the altars. We'd typically head home around 9 p.m. and spend the rest of our waking hours getting ready to return to "normal" life the next day.

Monday and Tuesday were devoted to school and work. Sometimes on Monday nights, we would participate in "Visitation," an activity that would involve visiting the visitors or the absentees from the day before. Wednesday night was the mid-week service. We had youth ministry services for the teenagers, Bible study for the adults, and children's classes for the grade school kids. For me, Thursday night was a young men's program called Royal Rangers. Friday and Saturday we were usually on our own with the occasional Saturday church event—picnics, door-to-door witnessing, etc. Growing up in this environment, the message I got was loud and clear—church is about being gathered and taught something. And we gathered a lot.

Honestly, we were sloppy about being sent (seeking). The regular activities were all about being gathered. Occasionally, we would engage in activities designed to get us out in the world to tell people about Jesus. Of course, we were constantly encouraged to bring "unsaved" people to our services. I did my best to get my friends to join me at church. Once in a while, I would succeed in spending all my relational equity with a friend and they would come with me to a church gathering. It was quite a cultural shock for most of them. They would usually be kind and never come back. It was awkward and discouraging, to say the least.

More often, being sent meant going on a "missions trip" to another country and assisting the missionaries there. We'd typically spend several days holding open-air meetings, doing puppet shows for kids, or going door to door inviting people to come to nightly meetings. Rarely would we do any of these things back home. For the most part, being *sent* literally meant getting on a plane and crossing an ocean.

Version 2.0 of the 20th-century church was less of more of the same. Most churches had one weekly service (typically on Sunday morning). Period.

The more active ones threw in a small group and/or a mid-week gathering. The emphasis was on the priority of being the gathered (saving) church, and the scorecard of what constitutes a thriving church stayed the same—how many show up every week to hear the carefully scripted message, skillfully delivered in 35 minutes or less.

The problem is that all this focus on being the gathered church meant that half of our missional purpose was being neglected. The societal results were stunning. "According to data from the latest version of the Public Religion Research Institute's annual 'American Values Atlas,' 25 percent of Americans today are religiously unaffiliated, up from single digits in the 1990s. Among young people, that number is 39 percent."[25] If the Church insists on continuing on our merry way making our gatherings the main event, we appear to be on pace toward ceasing to exist in one generation. It's true. The COVID crisis dramatically disrupted this "gathered" church focus. But way too many churches simply rode out the crisis and worked hard to get back to their comfort zone in the gathering place.

The 21st-century church built on a platform of discipleship will need to develop a whole new set of habits. As we already discussed, broadband discipleship involves seeking AND saving. The 21st-century church is sent to seek and gathered to save. It's both/and, not either/or. This will have significant implications for the habits of the 21st-century church. Here are some habits that will become normal in the 21st-century church.

21ST-CENTURY CHURCH HABITS

Church calendar built around missional activities. For example, one week the church may sponsor a small group for the purpose of assisting

---

25   https://www.getreligion.org/getreligion/2019/7/28/hazel-motes-do-not-pray-for-us

disciples with spiritual formation. The opposite week disciples are sent out to participate in community-sponsored meet-ups so the church can be in proximity to those who are being sought by Jesus.

Holistic disciple-making practices. Disciple-making-oriented metrics will take into account the entire process of discipleship from initial encounter with a Christ follower to a multiplying disciple. For example, counting and celebrating spiritual conversations should be as important as taking attendance at the weekly public gatherings. The number of intentional faithful prayers for neighbors and acquaintances should be just as important as how much money is being received in the offering plate (or through the offering app).

Fewer Church-centric gatherings. For most churches, the habit pattern will mean fewer gatherings and more people being sent. Some church calendars are so packed with gatherings that the parishioners possess little bandwidth to have their neighbors over to share a meal.

Spiritual formation on mission. Spiritual formation on mission will replace fill-in-the-blank discipleship programs. An example of spiritual formation on mission would be a disciple serving as a big brother/big sister for a troubled youth, checking regularly with his/her spiritual mentor to debrief what he/she is learning from the role of big brother/big sister.

Better use of face-to-face time. The necessity for taking ministry online during the COVID crisis had at least one important outcome. We all discovered that some things are best done online—specifically teaching and training. Many 21st-century churches are now using online forums to deliver their teaching/training content and reformatting their face-to-face meetings for activities that are best done face to face. Scripture refers to them as the "one another's." Here's a non-exhaustive list of actions that are best done when we are together face to face.

- Be devoted to one another
- Honor one another
- Live in harmony with one another
- Accept one another
- Greet one another
- Agree with one another
- Encourage one another
- Be kind and compassionate toward one another
- Bear with one another
- Speak to one another
- Submit to one another
- Love one another
- Pray for one another
- You get the point.

The best way for a church to form 21st-century habits is to start with them in the first place. The adage "you can't teach an old dog new tricks" most certainly applies here. It is really difficult for a worshipping community that has settled into 20th-century habits to change. This is why starting new churches guided by 21st-century guidelines is so important. New churches guided by 21st-century principles will have a much greater probability of long-term missional effectiveness than new churches started on a 20th-century platform.

But what about existing churches? Can they transition from 20th-century habits to 21st-century habits? My best answer is perhaps. Here's how a 20th-century church leader might develop 21st-century habits.

1. Practice being a 21st-century Christian—meet your neighbors, have them over for a meal, help them follow Jesus, help them grow in Christ and help others follow Jesus.
2. Start with a guiding coalition. Invite them to do the same.
3. Keep the normal habits going.
4. When the 21st-century Christians become the 2/3 majority, then perhaps you've made the transition.

Alternatively, consider sending out experiments into the harvest. Instead of trying to change the church you lead, send out a catalytic leader with the mandate to raise up a worshipping community built on 21st-century principles. Either way, the mission of Christ and the lost who need to be sought win.

The focus of this chapter has been on the "how" of being a fruitful 21st-century church. Habits must change. How we be the Church will be modified. But we won't get the "how" right if we don't get the "why" right. The "why" will be the focus of our next shift.

IN THEIR OWN WORDS...

Eric and Sarah Hoke, are the founders and key leaders for All Saints Church, which serves the Concourse Village neighborhood of the Bronx, New York.

Please share a brief synopsis of your vocational and ministry experiences BEFORE you began the process of starting this new church.

Prior to launching my own church, I worked on staff at two different medium-sized, well-established churches. One church was in rural New Jersey and shared land with a cornfield and one was in Queens, New York —the most diverse county in the world and one of NYC's five boroughs. One church was a traditional Pentecostal church complete with the altars in front of the sanctuary, an army of volunteers who ran the million programs and rust-orange carpet in the auditorium that looks like it had been there for 50 years. The other church was also about 150 people and much more modern, the pastor wore blue jeans and untucked button-downs, he preached off a pub table and worked hard to make the sermons relevant. We met in a movie theater and began unloading our truck of supplies every Sunday at 7 a.m. and after two services and tear-down, I was happy to be home by 5 p.m. The congregation was mostly young families and singles. I learned so much from both churches and am indebted to my time and mentorship in both congregations.

Please share a brief summary of the start-up process of your church thus far.

Our church plant is three years old post-launch, excluding a year of "Year 0" which was forming relationships with people in the community and building the groundwork for planting a viable congregation. Our church is located in the Bronx, New York.

With the shift of this chapter in mind, describe the process of your own journey.

We struggle with many of the same temptations Steve outlines above—mistakenly subscribing to faulty thinking that says more church activity = progress + mission. The new shift that I recognized during my formation as a church planter came in a leadership workshop I attended where the facilitator gave what he shared as a throwaway comment that stuck in my spirit: "People will naturally take care of one another, they will not naturally go on mission."

This hit me like a ton of bricks because I realized, yes, that is spot-on. People in our church have no problem praying with each other post-service, grabbing brunch together once we are done with teardown, or hosting game nights or small groups in one another's homes. Caring for people in your church family is natural for most Christians because they have been conditioned that this is what the church does.

However, when you're a church plant first starting out, this can become an Achilles heel, if that is all we do. We become one big happy family, which for many people, that is what church is, and that is all that church is and all that church should be. One way I aim to temper the care for one another with sharing the good news is that I try to end each sermon with, "Who can you bring Christ to this week?" or "Who can you share this message with?" or "Who wasn't sitting here today that needs this Word—could God be calling you to bring it to him or her?"

One creative way we did that was during the COVID-19 crisis. The Bronx was the hardest-hit community in the hardest-hit city in the world. At the time of this writing, no one in my church has died of COVID-19, but everyone knows someone who has died. One of the biggest losses for our church was job loss, and in a matter of four weeks from March to April 2020, half of our church lost their jobs and income.

We decided to do something different and gave every person in our church $100 with no agenda other than to bless themselves or someone else in Jesus' name. We also supported larger organizations fighting COVID-19 in New York City. That one Sunday, we gave away about $4,000, which is 5 percent of our annual operating budget! We believed God was calling us to step out in faith and be about the mission. That was not easy, especially as were not having in-person gatherings and our internal giving was down.

We could have used that money to hold a huge event at our church post-COVID, we could have done a block party or big blowout in a park, we could have done a large "come and see" event, but we decided to swap that out for a "go and be" experience—equipping our people to live on mission and to care for those in their lives with the love of Christ.

Anything else you'd like to share?

"Our first year as a church plant, we did many traditional evangelism efforts that I was conditioned to do in my previous churches. We did block parties with big bounce houses and BBQs with all the goodies to choose from. We dumped more money than I care to admit into mailers and passed out flyers for church to rushed commuters going to the subway. In our first year, we spent $10,000 on "outreach" items like these, only to have exactly... zero people ever show up to church. Talk about disheartening.

Our team went back to the drawing board and talked through creative ways to engage our neighbors in areas they would find helpful and enjoyable. We found most of our outreach strategy was transactional—if we feed you a hot dog or let your kid bounce in this bounce house, you'll come to our church, right? Well, not in the South Bronx.

We decided to change our approach to create experiences that added value to the lives of people in our community and if they got plugged into our faith community long term, that was a nice add-on.

One idea that was hatched from this shift was hosting an event called "Bronx-trepreneur" which was a play on words, Entrepreneurs from The Bronx. We knew that there were several creative, start-up-minded people living in our community who were working hard to get their small businesses off the ground and who could benefit from a workshop like this. We had no idea what would come of it, but we just went for it and hoped for the best. I remember one time saying, "If 50 people come to this, that would be insane!"

We had a local businessman give a keynote speech, we had live music, a taco bar, and a T-shirt giveaway. Because we rent our worship space, we only have access to it on Sunday mornings at 11 a.m., which is when we held our event. I know some people would crawl in their skin to "take away from the word" on a Sunday morning but that is what we did.

About 150 people came to Bronx-treprenuer, blowing my expectations out of the water, and dozens came back to our church in the coming months. At the time of this writing, we still have several people who attend All Saints who were introduced to our church at Bronx-treprenuer.

SHIFT TEN

RECONSIDER CORE VALUES

From Institution-Focused to Mission-Oriented.

During his career as a teacher and college professor, besides actually teaching classes, my father was involved in training aspiring actors. Many of his students went on to careers in Hollywood and on Broadway. But they got their start under the skillful tutelage of my father. My dad always found ways for his children to be involved in the plays his students performed. I ran lights, played minor roles, moved props around, etc. I spent a lot of time around live theater environments and, without really realizing it at the time, absorbed a lot of knowledge about the skill of acting.

One of the most important things that separates good actors from great ones is understanding the motivation that moves their character to action. Great actors internalize these motivations, so they literally feel them when they are "in character." Feeling the motivation enables them to authentically portray their character. Thus, the question, "What's my motivation?"

Motivation matters a lot. An actor needs to understand the motivation of the character to successfully become that character. Accurately knowing and authentically feeling the motivations of the character leads to a believable acting performance. In fact, the same action prompted by different motivations will look very different to the audience viewing the performance. The audience sees a hug. But is that hug motivated by greed, lust, affection, rage, etc.? The hug will be believable only to the degree that it is consistent with the motivation of the character as internalized by the actor.

"What's my motivation?" is the question that underlies what are commonly referred to as *value statements*. Vision and mission statements answer the "what" and "how" questions. But value statements are a declaration of "why" we do what we do—the "What's my motivation?" question. Every church needs to answer the "What's my motivation?" question carefully, because the motivation will greatly impact the perceived authenticity and meaning of the actions they take. Why are we doing what we do? Why do we have Sunday School? Why do we gather for worship weekly? Why do we intentionally participate in city council meetings? Why do we fight for justice? Why do we advocate for the oppressed and underserved? Why do we give to missions? These questions all get at the motivation behind specific actions. And the motivation of why we do what we do will have a significant impact on the outcomes of our actions.

For example, a church gives generously to missions works around the world. That's an action. But what's their motivation? Duty? Compassion? Habit? Pride? Humility? It's crucial to understand that the same action can have different motivations, and those motivations matter a lot.

As the Denver Seven journeyed together building contextually appropriate communities of faith in seven distinct city neighborhoods, the need to get the "why" right became crystal clear. They quickly discovered that many of the plug-and-play core values that motivated the 20th-century church are completely unhelpful in the 21st-century context.

For the remainder of this chapter we will look at some of the 20th-century core values the Denver Seven found necessary to reconsider for the 21st century.

CORE VALUE SHIFT I: FROM BIBLE CENTRIC TO GOSPEL CENTRIC

Think about it. The early church did not have the Bible to read. No "read through the Bible in a year" plans. No "turn with me to the fourth chapter of Luke" sermon comments. No pocket New Testaments. No questions about the tension between Paul and Peter's writings. Most of the New Testament was being written while the events of Acts were playing out. The fact is that until Gutenberg's press, the scriptures were mainly passed along verbally. Which means that during the time of its most explosive growth, the people of the Church did not have immediate access to the written words of scripture. And yet, somehow the Church managed to go from a scared huddle of demoralized disciples to being recognized as the religion of the entire Roman Empire in three centuries. This is especially remarkable when you consider that Christianity was born into a religious cultural soup that contained hundreds of little sects and minor religions all competing for the attention of the citizens of Rome. How did Christianity win? Rodney Stark takes a crack at this question in his book *The Rise of Christianity*. His conclusion says it all. "Christianity did not grow because of miracle working in the marketplaces (although there may have been much of that going on), or because Constantine said it should, or even because the martyrs gave it such credibility.... the primary means of its growth was through the united and motivated efforts of the growing numbers of Christian believers, who invited their friends, relatives, and neighbors to share the "good news."[26] This all happened without easy access to the Bible.

The 20th-century church highly valued the Bible as the platform on which everything stands. But just like the church of the earliest centuries, the 21st-century church will discover the pure power of the Gospel and the story of Jesus to change the hearts and souls of people far from God. I am aware that this concept will be viewed by some as controversial, perhaps bordering on the edge of heresy. But I urge you to pause for a moment to consider what I believe will be a key harbinger of success of the 21st-century church—will we insist that people believe in the Bible before they can believe in Jesus? Because, for many, that's how it felt in the 20th century. "The Bible Says..." was viewed as the trump card in every spiritual conversation. "The Bible Says..." works well when people respect the Bible as the Word of God. But in a culture that is increasingly irreligious, insisting that people begin with accepting the Bible as God's Word is a serious obstacle to them knowing Jesus.

Jesus Himself understood this. In an encounter with the Jewish religious leaders, he said,

"You study the Scriptures diligently because you think that in them you have eternal life. These are the very Scriptures that testify about me, yet you refuse to come to me to have life."27

Jesus literally puts the scriptures in their place by reminding the religious leaders that the purpose of scripture is to testify about Jesus. Jesus is the beginning and the end. He needs to be the beginning and the end in the 21st-century church as well.

---

26   Rodney Stark, The Rise of Christianity, Harper Collins, page 208
27   John 5:39-40 (NIV)

This is why it is crucial for the 21st-century church to begin with Jesus, not the Bible. Starting with Jesus first worked out well for the early church, and He is the right place to start for the 21st-century church.

CORE VALUE SHIFT 2: FROM MONOETHNIC TO MULTICULTURAL

It's a well-known concept that 11 a.m. to noon on Sunday is the most segregated hour of the week. Despite that being the observation/complaint for decades, it has remained an unfortunate reality of the gathered church. At first glance, the adage "birds of a feather flock together" appears to apply to the gathered church as much as it does to any other sector of society. In fact, disturbingly, way too often, it seems to apply more so.

Part of the reason mono-ethnicity became a 20th-century guiding value was a pragmatic and well-intentioned concept that emerged in the 20th century commonly referred to as the "Homogeneous Unit Principle." The H.U.P. was introduced by missiologist Donald McGavran during the heyday of the Church Growth Movement. The basic underlying idea of the H.U.P. is embodied in the following sentence: "People like to become Christians without crossing racial, linguistic or class barriers."[28] The H.U.P. has inspired many passionate debates about its implications for the Church and whether or not it is even ethical. Regardless of your opinion on the H.U.P., its impact on starting and strengthening churches is undeniable. Most of the church-starting and strengthening strategies that emerged in the 20th century had the H.U.P. as a core value motivating their strategies.

As the 21st century dawned, new voices began to arise in support of a different core value. Proponents like Mark DeYmaz[29] began to suggest that the

---

28   https://journals.sagepub.com/doi/
abs/10.1177/239693937800200102?journalCode=ibmb
29   https://books.google.com/books/about/Building_a_Healthy_Multi_ethnic_Church.
html?id=KE_JhkOEh3AC&printsec=frontcover&source=kp_read_button#v=onepage&q&f=-
false

local church would better represent the Church that Jesus is building if she were guided by a core value of intentional diversity. Calls began to be heard for the emergence of local churches that "look like heaven." We are now seeing a trend toward more intentionality toward fostering a church culture that is welcoming to diverse people from every imaginable category of diversity.

Whatever you think of the H.U.P. or the trend to more intentionality toward multicultural congregations and church start-up strategies, it does indeed appear that 21st-century culture is rapidly diversifying and churches that thrive in the 21st century will reflect that diversity. Continuing to exist as homogenous cultural islands in the midst of a diversifying general culture is not an option for a thriving church. An awareness of the need for the Church to "look like heaven" is growing amongst church leaders everywhere. Tolerance for mono-ethnic worship environments is fading fast and being replaced by desires and actions that encourage people of all ethnicities, economies, and political persuasions to subjugate their identities to a Kingdom-first identity.

This is way easier said than done. Long, deep prejudices and perspectives, economic inequalities, institutionalized racism, and political animosities stand ready to sabotage any efforts to bring diverse people together. Society has painfully learned the shortcomings of solving prejudice and racial divides through legislation, investment. and social justice movements. The truth is that these well-intended efforts to push back the specter of ugly racial hate are only putting a Band-Aid on the problem. In the end, the hate is still there, pushing people apart. It's ironic then that the Church Jesus is building is at the same time the only real solution to the cancer of racism and economic exploitation and the most obvious symptom of the fact that we have a long way to go.

The Church of the 21st century will be the church that demonstrates prophetically and in practice a society where there is no Jew or Gentile, slave or free, male or female, etc. The city is the school of hard knocks where the Church is learning to look like heaven. Why? Because citizens of the city have no choice but to learn to get along with people who are different from them. Or be miserable, unsafe, or just leave for a mono-cultural haven somewhere else.

City churches, especially newer ones, are, out of necessity, discovering what it looks like when the church becomes the place where all other identities are subject to the identity of the Kingdom of God. In God's Kingdom, the Oneness that Jesus prayed for in John 15 becomes an imperfect but living reality authentically uniting people who have been divided by the prejudices of man. City churches that thrive are intentionally seeking to align their behaviors with the classless society of heaven. Churches that look like heaven are not the norm yet, but they will be on the increase from now until the end of the age.

The underlying motivations (values) of the emerging multi-ethnic, economic, and politically diverse urban churches result in some common crucial characteristics that every healthy 21st-century church will do well to pay attention to.

HEALTHY HABITS OF CULTURALLY DIVERSE CHURCHES.

- They facilitate ongoing conversation about ethnic perspectives. People of various ethnic and economic backgrounds meet intentionally to learn from each other.
- They support intentional mentoring relationships between minority culture and dominant culture disciples.

- They are intentional about having leaders from diverse backgrounds on their platforms and in their organizational leadership teams.
- They demonstrate consistent prioritization of Kingdom culture over every other culture while at the same time appropriately celebrating the attributes of the diverse cultures.
- They seek out and support the best practices of economic justice.
- They proactively attack economic illiteracy.
- They exercise their influence on behalf of economically exploited people.
- They wade into the complexity of gentrification and bring the voice of biblical justice and compassion into the conversation.
- They speak prophetically against those who oppress the poor for selfish gain.
- They adopt a politically neutral stance, reminding everyone that Jesus has hard things to say to both parties.
- They encourage people of faith to use the political system to influence the collective culture toward Kingdom values.
- They keep the worship gatherings as political free zones so that people from all political perspectives can worship God together.
- They train Kingdom citizens how to hold strong political views and love those who differ with them.

CORE VALUE SHIFT 3: FROM SEPARATION TO REDEMPTION

The other day I received a call from a friend of mine who serves as the pastor of a local church in a very conservative part of the nation. He was looking for counsel on how he could best serve a same-sex couple that had started attending the church he leads. We had a great conversation and I was reminded once again of the dramatic contrasts between ministry in the 20th century and the 21st century.

The core value of the 20th-century church was separation. Perhaps the theme verse was "'Come out from them and be separate,' says the Lord."[30] This value of separation manifested itself in things like recreation centers where Christians could work out and not have to hear the foul language or view the inappropriate attire of non-Christians. The goal of outreach was to get people to come into our church buildings (our comfort zone) so they could hear the message. Even when we succeeded at getting pagans into our buildings dedicated to the glory of God, we expected sinners to immediately straighten up and fly right.

Years ago, I was serving as a youth pastor at a very strong 20th-century church and doing my best to bring "unsaved" young people to church meetings at our building. Few youths in this particular community had access to cars or even reliable public transportation, so we overcame that obstacle by sending out buses to pick them up and bring them to our building. It was quite messy. Fights in the parking lot, marijuana smoking in the restrooms, language in the church hallways that would make a sailor blush. Word of the chaos got back to one of the deacons, who promptly pulled me aside and told me that I should have a policy of bringing "bus kids" two times. If they did not accept Jesus as Lord and Savior after the first two visits, then they should not be allowed to ride the bus to church. Thankfully, cooler heads prevailed, and that policy was never enacted. But just the fact that it was even considered as an option demonstrates the short-sightedness of some 20th-century values.

In the 21st century, the 20th-century guiding value of "separation" is giving way to the value of redemption or living redemptively. Living

---

30   2 Corinthians 6:17 NIV

redemptively means that we start with a firm foundation of surrender to Christ and the empowerment of His Spirit. As Spirit-empowered followers of Jesus, we live like Him in proximity to our neighbors, co-workers, class-mates, and other acquaintances that our normal lives bring us into contact with. Relying firmly on the Lord's strength, we do indeed keep ourselves separate from sin, but we live confidently out in the world bringing the peace, truth, and love of God into every sector of culture and society.

The 20th-century value of separation was intended to honor God, but it had the unintended consequence of isolating Christians from the very people Jesus is seeking. For many, church became a place of refuge from that evil world out there, instead of a launching pad to be sent out to join Jesus in his redemptive work. The calendar of many churches became so filled up with sanctified "church" activities that followers of Jesus had little time for anything but spending time with each other.

21st-century churches and Christians will need to rediscover the art of cultivating redemptive relationships with people who are different from us. People who disagree with us. People who practice lifestyles that make us feel uncomfortable and whom we think are wrong. We are going to need to be willing to be outside of our comfort zones, engaging with those around us in contexts where they feel at home.

Moving from separation to redemptive relationships will be messy. Without the protective walls of controlled environments around us, we will need to learn how to experience the empowerment of the Holy Spirit in fresh ways. We will need to listen more than we talk. When we speak, we will need to learn to trust the Holy Spirit to give us redemptive words of truth and grace.

Like my pastor friend who is seeking the path of grace and truth with the same-sex couple attending his very conservative church, we will find ourselves dealing with increasingly complex societal attitudes and values that will often be at odds with our understanding of Kingdom values.

The ongoing question for the 21st-century church will be "How will we respond to those around us redemptively with grace and truth?"

Here are some of the questions 21st-century leaders will need to be prepared to answer for people they are leading toward Jesus.

- How do we reconcile the Kingdom value of generosity with the emotions of fear and greed that drive capitalism?

- How does the God of the Old Testament align with the Jesus of the New Testament?

- How will the church respond to my transgender child?

- How will the church involve herself in matters of social justice?

- How will individuals who identify with the LGBTQ community be welcomed into the spiritual journey of the church?

CORE VALUE SHIFT 4: FROM LOCATION TO PROXIMITY

The 20th-century formula for success was location, location, location. In fact, many 20th-century churches were started simply because a great location was available. The right location meant ample parking, easy access from the nearest interstate or major highway, great facility, and worship-conducive meeting space. Once the right location was identified, it was just a matter of letting people know that a fantastic new church would be meeting there soon and before you know it, a church pops out. Okay, I'm exaggerating just a little bit. But only a little bit!

The assumptions of the 20th-century formula were things like:

1. Everyone will be traveling to the location via automobile.

2. Most people will be willing to travel a long way to experience a high-quality worship environment.

3. Adequate parking is of the utmost priority. Parking lot attendants are a necessity.

When location, location, location was the value, rapidly growing new suburban housing developments were the prize. It was not uncommon for a new suburb to have multiple new church-starting teams all looking for space in the brand-new school, movie theater, or freshly built community center to start their new church in. I wish I had a dollar for every time I received a call from a prospective church starter letting me know that God was calling him or her to the latest, greatest, brand-new, rapidly growing suburban community. Don't get me wrong. Sparkly new subdivisions need new churches too. And, for a lot of legitimate reasons, newly relocated citizens are typically more receptive to the idea of a new church.

Ironically, in location-based new church-starting, the actual location is not as important as the amenities of the location—primarily, does it comfortably accommodate a lot of people traveling by car?

In the 21st century, the word "location" is being replaced by the value of "proximity." The places where the church is thin tend to be places where the available locations are not convenient for people traveling by car. 21st-century church-starting will be about increasing the presence of the Church in the places that are hard. In the 20th century, the need for the leader to live in the same community as the meeting location was not significant. In the 21st century, the need for the leader to live in the community is mission critical. This is proving to be true whether it is in the hard-scrabble urban hoods, the upscale hipster havens, or the vertical neighborhoods downtown. The inspiration for the shift toward the priority of "proximity" is the profound statement John makes about Jesus in his Gospel. "The Word became flesh and blood and moved into the neighborhood..." John 1:14 (The Message). Jesus, who being in very nature God, became one of us, that we might know Him. The next frontier for the Church is for us to become one of "them" so that they might know Him.

This idea of proximity being primo has become real to me as I've lived in an urban neighborhood, known in Denver as Uptown. Over time, I've become acquainted with an increasing number of my neighbors. I've prayed with them, had numerous faith conversations with them, and even had the joy of seeing some of them come to faith. These are busy people who have zero interest in finding their way out to a suburban church with a large parking lot. Some of them don't even have cars! The only way many of my neighbors will ever have a thoughtful encounter with a disciple of Jesus is for that person to "move into the neighborhood" and be one of them.

As the urbanization of America continues, urban-like living experiences are going to be on the increase. People living in these places typically value walking and public transportation over traveling by car. An increasing number of young people are choosing Uber and Lyft over a driver's license. It won't happen overnight, but the need for neighborhood-focused communities of faith is going to grow over time.

One final thought about location and proximity. Location-based churches are best in settings where people tend to be spread out and don't mind driving their cars to get to church. The core philosophy is to create a great destination experience and draw people from as far and wide as possible. In nature, tending to move toward a center is called *centripetal force*. The core philosophy of "proximity"-based churches is to start at a center and move out from there, which is called *centrifugal force*. Centrifugal churches will become more and more common as every place becomes increasingly missiologically challenging.

CORE VALUE SHIFT 5: FROM EXCELLENCE TO OBEDIENCE

Pause for a minute and Google the phrase "we value excellence church." Go ahead, I'll wait until you get back..........

Google gave me 49,000,000 results in less than a second. You probably got something similar. You also probably saw links to the websites of some really great churches. Some of you started surfing those websites and forgot to come back to the book. I get it. Excellence is a good value to have. It's actually rare for a church NOT to list excellence as a core value.

Excellence was perhaps the most common church core value of the 20th century. I'm a fan of excellence. Everything should be done with excellence as a guiding principle. Everything. Work hard at it, fight for it. It does matter. People need to know that you are not throwing things together at the last minute. Excellence is first and foremost until it stands in the way of something far more crucial: obedience.

The 21st-century church will carefully keep obedience as a primary value. What is God calling us to do? That's the obedience question. Sometimes, in fact perhaps normally, his call pushes us toward something we are certain we cannot do with excellence. Such a situation creates a values conflict and unfortunately, too often, excellence subtly wins over obedience. For the church to be effectively on Mission with Jesus, we are going to find ourselves increasingly called to go to places where commitment to excellence will need to bow to our determination to obey the directives of the Lord. Hearing God's call to go to the hard places will bring on this value clash hard and fast.

Too often, the conversation sounds something like this....

The Lord says: "Go to the underserved community and be my Church in that neighborhood."

We respond: "We have no experience in places like that, Lord. Our way of being the Church won't work there."

The nooks and crannies of culture underserved by the Church are going to be hard for us to go to. We won't know how to go well, and if excellence is our first priority, then we won't go to those places at all and the Gospel risks being bottled up in the places we know we can be excellent.

So, be obedient first. Then learn how to be excellent. That's the right order for the 21st-century church.

In this chapter we've looked at some of the core value adjustments our Denver Seven discovered must take place for the Church to be effective in the 21st century. This list is certainly not exhaustive. It may be wise for you and your leadership team to take some time to reflect on other values shifts that you may need to make to be effective in the 21st-century context.

One value shift we did not discuss in this chapter is so critical that it deserves an entire chapter of its own. It's the shift from addition to multiplication. That shift will be the focus of our next chapter!

IN HER OWN WORDS....

Dr. Eleanore Kue MD, founder, His Healing Hands Urgent Care Clinic and Healing Hands Church, Lansing, Michigan

The values that have guided your life have helped you achieve extraordinary accomplishments. Tell us your story of following Jesus wherever he leads.

I was born in Cameroon, Central Africa. Because my country was colonized by France, I grew up speaking French. When I was 16 years old, my parents sent me to France to study medicine. While in Cameroon, I attended a church, but I didn't have a relationship with Jesus. I believed in God; however, I didn't think He was interested in me. I felt I was responsible for my own life.

As a medical student In France, I was busy studying and went to church sparingly. My church life didn't affect my "real" life. I didn't read the Bible and only prayed emergency prayers before exams or when I needed help. God became a vending machine to me.

I married my high school sweetheart, Simon Kue, in 1992, and we flew to the U.S. for our honeymoon. The best man in our wedding was living in the U.S. already and had invited us. I like to say that for our honeymoon, we went to a place where few people go: Huntsville, Alabama. My husband immediately fell in love with America, the land of opportunity. We went back to France, applied for permanent visas, packed, and moved to the United States.

I learned English and went back to complete a second residency. I received my board certification in dermatology in France and became board certified in preventive and occupational medicine in the U.S. While attending school and learning a new specialty, two of our children were born. I became busy as a wife, mother, and student without church involvement.

Ten years into our American dream, we looked successful according to societal standards. I was a physician working for General Motors, married to a pharmacist. We had three children by then and lived in an upscale neighborhood. I had more than I could have ever dreamt of, but my life was empty. Our marriage became destructive, and I had no joy. I began to wonder what the meaning of life was. In my quest for answers, I went back to what I knew. I started looking for a church for myself and in which to raise my children. On a random Saturday afternoon, in the bathroom of my children's music school, a lady who later became my friend invited me to an Assembly of God church.

In 2002, I walked into First Assembly of God of East Lansing, Michigan, for the first time. I immediately felt love, accepted, and at home. I was so drawn to the people that I began to attend church five times a week. My hunger for the Bible grew and I decided to attend a local Bible institution. I went to Bible school because I wanted to learn about the Bible. I didn't know what it meant to be called and I didn't know if it was for me. I was introduced to missions while in Bible school. We had missionaries from around the world come and speak to us, some even coming from Africa. After the first quarter, I wanted to experience missions for myself. In 2006, my family and I went on an adventure, a mission trip to Panama where I served as the team physician. The following year our church sent my husband and I with a team of health care professionals on a medical mission trip to Cameroon. It was on this trip in 2007 that God spoke to me and sent me home to Lansing with a desire to do what we were doing on the mission field—open a clinic for the uninsured and underinsured in my own community. I subsequently resigned from my job as an attending physician in a major hospital in 2009 and opened His Healing Hands Clinic in Lansing, Michigan. I obeyed God, not knowing what I was getting into.

Shortly after I opened the clinic, I became overwhelmed by my patients' stories. My patients were largely from the surrounding community, inner-city Lansing, and struggled with drug addiction, domestic abuse, homeless, unemployment, were ex-convicts, etc. They were living in anguish and were hopeless. I so desperately wanted to share the hope that I found in Jesus. Praying with them in the exam room was not enough. I started inviting my patients to Bible study on Thursdays for a deeper immersion into the Word of God, which has the power to save, heal, and deliver. The Thursday meetings grew and in 2013, I planted a church at the clinic. The church grew! More patients voiced their desire to come to church. A friend donated an eight-passenger van to us and my daughter began busing adults and children from the housing projects around Lansing to our church at the clinic. Soon, we outgrew the clinic. It could hold only so many people, we could make only so many rounds to pick people up, and it was frankly no longer cost efficient.

When my daughter left for college, I was left with the responsibility of being both the bus driver and the pastor. It was then that I decided to take the church to them. I decided it would be best to go to the housing projects on Sundays, where there is already a community center, and have church where the people are. My dream was met with resistance from management, and I was told that because of the separation of church and state, I couldn't have church in the community centers of the public housing projects. I was disappointed but not discouraged. Every Sunday, I would set up church services in a nearby park by each housing project and have an outdoor church service. God blessed us with 22 Sundays of great weather. We never cancelled church.

But by November, it was too cold to meet outside. Determined to continue to disciple my congregation, I went into their homes on Wednesdays and Sundays. I was discipling 35 families every week.

It was then that God opened an amazing door. Through my involvement with Children Evangelist Fellowship, I met Tim Denney, an attorney who specializes in defending religious freedom. Tim filed a lawsuit against the City of Lansing Housing Commission to challenge their denial of our use of the community centers for religious services. We won the lawsuit, and the judge gave us permanent access to the community centers on the public housing projects. By this time, my team and I were bringing the good news to three different housing projects on Sundays, a refugee community on Mondays, and we were still having church at the clinic on Wednesday mornings. After each church service we served food donated by a local restaurant.

As a physician, God gave me access to the lives of the people from my community. I am known as a doctor who cares and loves them enough to speak into their lives. My goal has been to expand and reach more housing projects, but my challenges are many. My helpers are coming from different churches. I challenge them to work together regardless of denomination, social status, or race for the same purpose—to bring the Gospel to the least of these in our community.

Every Sunday and Monday, we knock on doors to invite individuals to church or at least have spiritual conversations with people in the community. We gather in the community center and have a child-oriented service. Children are the majority of my congregation. After church we feed them and send them home. I am starting a monthly leadership training for the adults. The purpose is to build up leaders from the community who will work alongside my team to take charge of the spiritual growth of their community.

SHIFT ELEVEN
RECOMMIT TO MULTIPLICATION
From addition to movement.

In the 1980s, I had the privilege of serving on the staff of a strong, growing church. The pastor was definitely not content to just maintain the status quo. The church calendar revolved around "Big Days." "Big Days" meant something out of the ordinary was going to be part of the worship experience. The idea was that "Big Days" gave regular attendees an excuse to invite their friends to come with them to church to see a musical, or a special music group, or an illustrated sermon, etc. We even would set public attendance goals to encourage members to play their part in getting people into the pews. Of course, every "Big Day" included a strong salvation message and invitation to decide to follow Jesus. The hope was that every time we set a new high-water mark, the average attendance would tend to be higher than before the "Big Day."

And, for the most part, this strategy worked. During my time on staff at the church, I saw the average attendance grow from 400 to 800 in just four years. Today, the church is a mega-church, regularly gathering thousands of people together to worship Jesus. Most pastors would love for the story of the church they lead to resemble the story of this "Big Day" church. Nothing wrong with that. It's truly a great church that we can learn much from. Especially about addition.

But one day something interesting happened that really got my attention. The pastor announced that in a couple of months we would be sending out two leaders to start two new churches. Both new churches would be within easy driving distance of the sending church. He encouraged people to seriously pray about helping with the start-up of these two new churches. At the time this announcement was being made, the sending church was averaging about 400. The day came for the new churches to have their opening days. The two new churches had about 50 attendees each. The existing church had about 400. Interesting. In one day, the missional impact (as measured by noses) of the sending church went from 400 to 500. And it happened when people were sent out. It happened when the church multiplied.

Addition was the way the church moved forward in the 20th century. The norm for every church was to stay focused on adding more and more people to the congregation. Running out of space? Build a bigger building. Almost anything was justified in the effort to get more people to walk through the church doors. I once heard an advertisement on the radio about a church where the pastor was going to live on the roof of the church building until the attendance of the church exceeded a certain number.

Addition strategies will simply not be adequate to face the missional challenges of the 21st century. Population growth coupled with a general decline in interest toward organized religion are conspiring to frustrate the best efforts of church leaders guided by a strategy of addition. The missional strategy of the 21st century must be multiplication.

The Denver Seven were determined from the start to make multiplication normal. But they quickly discovered that believing multiplication is the right thing is not equal to multiplication. Making multiplication a priority requires decisions, actions, and habits that are very different from an addition-based church.

MAKING MULTIPLICATION "NORMAL."

Multiplication was embedded into the lifestyle of the Early Church. For the earliest believers, multiplication was as natural as breathing. The way it happened was simple and easily transferable to the 21st-century reality. Disciples made disciples. Leaders made leaders. Church made churches.

DISCIPLES MAKE DISCIPLES.

Acts 11 provides a glimpse of the power of this principle. Luke tells us about "some men" from Cyprus and Cyrene who go to Antioch to take the Gospel to the Gentiles because the Gospel was being preached only to the Jews. They made disciples who made disciples of the Gentiles in Antioch and the church that emerged became the sending church of the Apostle Paul.

Some scholars speculate that these men were businesspeople who traveled to Antioch to conduct business. Whatever the case may be, disciples making disciples was so normative, Luke doesn't even bother to share the names of the men God used to start the disciple-making community in Antioch.

Churches that cultivate a culture of multiplication will be built around a habit of disciples making disciples. One of the few contemporary churches built exclusively on a platform of disciple-making is Hope Chapel in Kaneohe, Hawaii, founded by the legendary Ralph Moore. I got to see this firsthand back in the 1990s when we took our entire leadership team to Hawaii for a week to learn from Ralph and his team. I'll never forget being in a "Mini Church" (the Hope Chapel moniker for small groups) and asking them to share the story of that particular Mini Church. The leader started the story. "Well, I was in prison a year ago and the prison ministry team from Hope Chapel came to the prison and shared the Gospel. I thought I'd already heard it, but this time it made sense to me. When I got out of prison, I went to Pastor Ralph's new believers' class and learned how to make disciples. The people in this group are my first set of disciples and soon they will all have their own Mini Churches made up of disciples they've made." His story was confirmed by the other group members. Turns out they were all former inmates and each and every one was planning to assemble their own Mini Church. As I listened to them, it struck me that they didn't know any better. They all thought this is the way that Christians act. No wonder Hope Chapel is perhaps the most prolific multiplying church on the planet. Hundreds of thousands of disciples have been made through the daughter, granddaughter, great-granddaughter, great-great-granddaughter (and so on) churches that can trace their lineage back to a disciple originally made at Hope Chapel.

The platform of disciples making disciples who make disciples naturally led to leaders who make leaders. Paul told Timothy to entrust these things to faithful men who will pass them along to others. A culture of leadership development is an essential component of a church that catalyzes a multiplication movement. Multiplication simply will not happen without leadership, and leadership is always embodied in a person. Organizations do not lead. Leaders lead. Leaders learn to lead by leading. A healthy, intentional culture of leadership discovers, develops, and deploys leaders into the field of harvest.

LEADERS MAKE LEADERS.

I learned this principle firsthand during the process of starting my first church. I received a call from a young man who had been a member of one of the youth groups I served as a youth pastor. He told me that he thought God was calling him to start a new church and asked if I could help him prepare for the task. My first knee-jerk reaction was that he would not make a good church starter because at the time, he was a high school mathematics teacher. I promise I'm not prejudiced against high school math teachers, but the knowledge and skills necessary to be an effective math teacher seemed to be very different from the knowledge and skills needed to be a successful church starter.

But he was clearly a sharp individual, so rather than just tell him I thought he was crazy, I gave him a chance to demonstrate that he might indeed be wired to start a new church. I told him that I would love to have him join me on the team of the church I was starting, but I could not afford to pay him so he would have to raise his own support to come join our staff and be mentored by me. I honestly thought he would call me back in a year and say that he was unable to raise the necessary funding. Instead, he called me back in a few weeks and shared that he had raised adequate support for him to join our church staff and be mentored by me.

I was stunned and realized I had a new problem. This sharp leader and his wife were relocating to join our church leadership team and I had no idea what to do with him or how to be a good mentor. But I welcomed him to come and began to ask the Lord for wisdom as to how to be the best mentor possible for this gifted young man.

I realized that, while being able to raise funds was a very important skill for successful church-starting, there were other crucial behaviors and skill sets he would need to hone to be effective. I made a skill set/behavior list and then thought about what I could have him do that would help him to develop those skills. Leaders learn to lead by leading, so after considering my options, I settled on the idea of asking him to start a campus ministry at a local university that had never had a truly viable Christian campus ministry. The beauty of this assignment was that it was impossible for him to fail. No one else had succeeded in starting a campus ministry on this particular campus, so if he did not succeed, it would not be viewed as a full-blown failure.

When he arrived, we talked about the opportunity and he was thrilled to take it on. Wow, did he ever take it on. With very little input from me, he figured out how to start a brand-new, very viable and successful campus ministry on this campus in less than a year. He developed a strong leadership team that took ownership of every aspect of the campus ministry. I realized that he had demonstrated he did indeed have the skills and behaviors that predict success in the endeavor of starting a new church.

We sent him out to start a new church and the rest is history. Today that church is one of the most missionally effective churches in the state of Utah. The leader was discovered in the context of a structured yet organic leadership development process.

My observation has been that every effectively multiplying church is intentional about making disciples who make disciples and leaders who make leaders. Without those organizational habits at the core, it is difficult and perhaps even impossible for a church multiplication movement to emerge.

CHURCHES MAKE CHURCHES.

When a culture of disciple-making catalyzes a culture of leadership development, the foundation is laid for a robust culture of church multiplication to emerge. An often-overlooked passage in Romans 15 demonstrates how normal multiplication was to the early church. In verse 23, the Apostle Paul is wrapping up his letter to the Romans. He makes this very interesting statement. "But now that there is no more place for me to work in these regions, and since I have been longing for many years to visit you, I plan to do so when I go to Spain. I hope to see you while passing through and to have you assist me on my journey there, after I have enjoyed your company for a while."[31] It's easy to read right past the multiplication significance of these two verses. Paul's first statement is actually quite puzzling on the surface. He says, "...now that there is no more place for me to work in these regions..." The fact is that Paul had started churches in just a few of the major cities in the Eastern Mediterranean region. The claim that there was no more place for him to work is ridiculous until you look at the world through Paul's eyes. He understood the Gospel to be a potent seed that would sprout and multiply wherever it was planted. He had done the work of starting churches in key cities and he had such a confidence that the church would spread from the main cities to the surrounding ones that he considered his work in that region complete. He understood that healthy churches make more healthy churches. He then goes on to share that he plans to go to Spain. To Paul and his fellow church leaders, Spain was a somewhat mysterious place inhabited by Barbarians. It represented completely fresh soil for the seed of the Church to be planted in. This desire

---

31   Romans 15:23-24 NIV

of Paul to go where no one had gone before was emblematic of the normal impulse of the New Testament Church to plant, multiply, and then go to the next unreached place and people. Churches make churches and they do so by asking the question, "Who's missing?" For Paul, the answer to that question was the people in Spain. They needed the Church to come to them. The question is the same for the 21st-century church.

Who's missing? The answer to that question will lead us into the cultural nooks and crannies of our cities and towns where the voice of the Church is dim or even unknown. When we exegete these places where the presence of the Church is thin or missing, the answer to the next question—"How do the missing become the found?"—will often be the establishment of a new faith community custom built for the unique characteristics of that local culture. That is how the early church moved forward.

Who's missing? How do the missing become the found? Based on those questions, Paul decided he had done all he could do where he was and decided to go to Spain where the missing lived. If he had indeed made it to Spain, you can rest assured he would have answered the second question by starting churches in the key cities and letting the church multiply out into the surrounding communities.

The 20th-century picture of a great church was one church that grew bigger and bigger in one place. The 21st-century picture of a great church will be one church that expands her missional footprint by always asking and answering these two crucial questions: "Who's missing?" and "How do the missing become found?" The answer to those two questions will lead healthy 21st-century churches to begin new faith communities that effectively incarnate the Gospel into the nooks and crannies of communities.

The 21st-century church will agree with Paul and understand that the Gospel is a potent seed that will continue to expand through multiplication to other peoples and places.

Yeah, but how?

Here are some practical examples of how the 21st-century church can recommit to multiplication.

1. Every church can be intentional about making disciples who make disciples. waves 2 and 9 are applicable here. A disciple who is not actively making disciples is not yet a disciple. By definition, disciples make disciples. For many 20th-century churches, the minimum norm for a "disciple" was that they regularly attended the Sunday worship gathering. Disciples in the effective 21st-century church will cultivate a habit of being continually in the process of making disciples. When a church is made up of "serial" disciple-makers, it has the most important ingredient of a multiplication movement.

2. Every church can be intentional about forming leaders who make leaders. Layered on top of a platform of habitual disciple-making will be an intentional process for discovering, developing, and sending leaders. The 20th-century norm for church leaders was that the followers helped the leader accomplish his vision. The 21st-century norm is that leaders raise up other leaders to carry out God's collective vision for the local church and God's personal vision for each leader being developed. Some of the leaders who are developed will be called by God to start new faith communities that are laser-focused on finding the missing.

3. Every church can pray for God to show them who is missing. The key question for the 20th-century church was "How do we grow our

church?" The key question for the 21st-century church is "Who's missing?" Layered on top of a platform of disciples who make disciples and leaders who develop leaders will be a culture of seeking the missing. Every church can cultivate a habit of holy dissatisfaction with the fact that an increasing number of our fellow citizens are living with a distorted picture of God and His Church. Every church can choose not only to count the number of people seated in the pews or viewing online, but they can choose to count, pray for, and seek those who are missing.

4. Every church can pray for wisdom on how to help start new faith communities that help the missing become found. For the 20th-century church, the key question was "How do we get them to come to us?" The key question for the 21st-century church is "How will we take the Gospel to them?" The answer to that question will be different for every church, every context, and every community. But it is a crucial question for every church to ask. Some will be ready to act on multiplication immediately. Others will require more prep work. But searching for the missing through sending missional catalysts to start new communities of faith is not an optional endeavor for a church that desires to be healthy and fully engaged with Jesus on His Mission.

5. Every church can discover the guiding model for multiplication that best fits how they follow Jesus. The start-up process for most 20th-century churches was basically the same concept with different skins. The 20th-century concept was a) Find a called leader, b) Help them gather people and money to start holding services as quickly as

possible, c) Reach sustainability through tithes and offerings alone within three years or less. The complexity of the 21st century will require multiple guiding frameworks skillfully applied to the cultural context being reached. House church networks, missional communities, coffee house churches, dance churches, dinner churches, conversation circle churches, online churches, etc., etc. All of these will have different start-up processes, costs, benefits, and challenges.

Please notice that the list above are actions that ANY church can take, regardless of size, financial position, or stage of maturity. Our Denver Seven adopted a posture and practice of multiplication from the moment they moved into their neighborhood of focus. As they made disciples, developed leaders, looked for the missing, and sent leaders to find them, their collective impact spread beyond their immediate neighborhood. Simple forms of being the Church are much easier to multiply than complex and expensive forms of being the Church.

Here are some potential guiding models for 21st-century multiplication movements:

1. Send out catalyst leaders—churches may take their first steps toward a habit of multiplication by raising up and sending out called and anointed leaders. These raised-up ones may be missionaries to other nations, church starters in other communities, or church catalysts in a nearby cultural context that is different from the cultural context of the sending church.

2. Sponsor a new church start-up in a place where many are missing— stand-alone autonomous churches. Some churches may choose to pursue multiplication through a strategy of intentionally starting

new, autonomous faith communities empowered to multiply as they see fit. There may be a time frame where the sending church and the started church share finances and governance, but the ultimate goal is for the newly started church to self-sustain and self-govern as soon as possible so that it can multiply.

3. Multi-site startups happen when a strong church deliberately starts other locations that provide an ecclesiastical environment similar to that of the sending church for the missing that they find. Multi-site campuses/locations are not intended to become stand-alone autonomous churches, but rather they are structured to be organizationally linked to the sending church in perpetuity.

4. Multi-innovate—customized neighborhood-focused expressions. Traditional multi-site strategies tend to lean heavily on the effectiveness of the "brand" of the sending church. Multi-innovate approaches allow each site to develop its own unique identity that is appropriate for the cultural context where the site is located. A great example of this approach is the Tampa Underground. The Underground is a collective of diverse, micro-expressions of the Church, linked together by mission, creed, and passion.[32]

I hope your takeaway from this chapter is that multiplication must become normal again. It's not something that only large churches should be thinking about. Multiplication must be embedded into the healthy practice of the Church from disciples making disciples to churches making churches and everything in between. It's not normal for churches to be one and done. For the Great Commission to become the Great Reality, every church must have offspring who have offspring who have offspring.

---

32   https://www.tampaunderground.com/our-story-index/#story-welcome

Where do we start? I wonder what would happen if every suburban church selected one city neighborhood in the core city near them and one rural community within an hour of their church. Core urban neighborhoods and isolated rural communities are typically places where a lot of missing people may be found. Once these communities of focus are identified, what if the church began to research the unique realities of these specific locations and then pray about the best approach to find the missing? In some situations, a clone of the brand of the sending church might be the most appropriate approach. In other cases (perhaps more often than not), a more creative approach might be the right way to raise up a community of believers in the location of focus. My observation of the current state of the church in America is that most cities typically have strong "mega-churches" on their perimeter. From a strategic standpoint, I wonder what would happen if these mega-churches led the way in going to the hard places where the missing will be found. I'm convinced it could be the next strong step forward for the Church that Jesus is building.

But strategy will not be enough. This is, in fact, the Church that Jesus is building. If our multiplication strategies are reduced to growth formulas and ecclesiastical tactics, all of our best efforts will not be enough. We've got to renew our sense of dependence on the empowerment of God's Spirit. Otherwise, we will find ourselves starting organizations that are churches in name only. We've got to be sure we are joining Jesus in His mission to build His Church. That will be the subject of our next chapter.

IN THEIR OWN WORDS....

Pastor Steve Milazzo leads Bethlehem Assembly in Valley Stream, New York. Valley Stream is a community that sits right on the border of the borough of Queens, New York City. Here is Pastor Milazzo's story of becoming a church that plants churches.

https://www.bethlehemag.org

"I have been pastoring in the same church for 35 years. I began as a youth pastor and then slowly moved into the lead pastor role 26 years ago.

"I love my church and the truth is, I don't have horror stories of being mistreated by people or church splits or board issues.

"It has been a joy to be the pastor of a church that loves to give to missions, reach the lost, and see God at work in the lives of people.

"One day as I was praying and walking around the block on which the church facility is located, I sensed that God wanted me to do three things. First, to be a very generous pastor and give generously and consistently to missionaries and mission projects all over the world. At present, Bethlehem supports 112 missionaries and ministries around the world. Second, I sensed God directing me to raise up sons and daughters to plant and revitalize churches on Long Island. It has been a joy to come alongside men and women who sensed God calling them to plant and revitalize churches in several different communities on Long Island. Third, God challenged me to lead the church in a building project that included purchasing the entire square block around the present church facility. To say the least, purchasing property on Long Island is a daunting task.

"As Bethlehem continued to grow numerically, we began to face a great challenge for space. It was then that I had to decide. Do we relocate, build bigger, or go multi-site?

"After much prayer and deliberation, the leadership of Bethlehem concluded that it was both/and, not either/or. We chose a modified approach to building a larger campus facility along with a definite focus on multi-site expansion that we believe is both more economically healthy and certainly more biblical. We recognized that planting churches or starting multiple campuses required the leaders of the church to undergo some mind shifts. Looking back, I would say, there have been three shifts.

"The first shift was a shift of 'shared leadership.' Every multiplying leader must come to the place where he or she believes that shared leadership is exponentially more powerful than one person being the primary voice, decision-maker, and communicator. The second shift was "We are much better together." When a church community begins to see itself as resource to other communities and other outreaches, then the leadership begins to see God's provisional blessings as a means to reach more and more people outside its congregational reach. Bethlehem is now positioned and resourced to partner with leaders who have been called by God to go into other communities and plant new Gospel communities, in our case new satellite campuses. The third shift was "The local church can't fulfill the great commission and truly be as healthy as God intended it to be without a planting mindset." Even though it may seem easier to just keep doing what we are doing, in the long run we will never be as effective and efficient if we do not transition into a multiplying church.

"We have begun the process and we now have two campuses, with one more campus scheduled to begin later this year. It has been one of the most exciting journeys I have embarked on in many years. Bethlehem has worked with Urban Islands Project to recruit, train, and deploy couples who have a heart to reach the unchurched in and around Valley Stream and the east side of Queens. We have worked hard to instill into the multi-site model at Bethlehem a strong emphasis on building awareness, connection, discipleship, and leadership training to create an environment of deep outreach. Our campus in Rosedale has been built through outreaches and relationships with two public schools in the community. Our third campus is working with a local public school and several outreaches to build awareness, connections, and discipleship. We are also working with a local public school in another community because our mindset is to bring Gospel transformation to as many communities as we can. As God opens new doors, we are willing to walk through them one community at a time.

"Our metrics for success go far beyond just attendance and giving numbers. When we measure success, we measure it based on how many new connections, how many new relationships, and how many people have come to the new campuses from that local community.

"Each campus has been launched with a strong Bethlehem DNA of outreach, small groups, discipleship, and leadership training. Each campus has a strong support network from the Valley Stream campus (the original campus), and we are building a good foundation for future campuses. As I reflect on the years I have been the lead pastor at Bethlehem, I am convinced that our Lord and Savior will not ask me when I stand before him, "How big was your building." He will ask me, "Did you make disciples who reached lost people!"

SHIFT TWELVE
REACTIVATE SPIRIT DEPENDENCE
From duty and strategy to necessity.

T he Denver Seven were circled up for yet another cohort meeting. The conversations were always rich times of peer learning and interaction. The subject tonight was "time management." The cohort facilitator asked each leader around the table to share a summary of how they spend their time each day of the week. As the sharing proceeded around the circle, it was clear that these leaders were taking the "seeking" side of discipleship very seriously. "On Mondays I work out at the same gym and meet new people every week." "Tuesdays are my civic leader days. I do a ride-along with the police and check in with our councilman to see if we can do anything to help him lead well." "Every day starts at the coffee shop."

Then it was Nathan Kwansah's time to share. Nathan immigrated to the United States from Nigeria. He received his master's in theology from Denver Seminary. Now he was in the process of starting a new church for first-generation immigrants from African nations. Nathan summed up his time management simply and concisely: "On Mondays we pray, on Tuesdays we pray, on Wednesdays we pray..." Every day, Nathan and his team prayed.

After everyone had shared their basic schedules, the facilitator asked everyone to share something they had learned from the exercise. Nathan quickly acknowledged how he would modify his schedule. "I need to go to the coffee shop." Everyone else responded with "I need to pray more." They were right, of course, but perhaps not the way you might think.

In 2018, Dr. Ed Stetzer wrote a great article on the "business" of church planting. In the article he notes that "church planting has become a multi-million-dollar business." He references an unknown source who suggests this:

"The Gospel came to the Greeks, and the Greeks turned it into a philosophy.

The Gospel came to the Romans, and the Romans turned it into a system.

The Gospel came to the Europeans, and the Europeans turned it into a culture.

The Gospel came to America, and the Americans turned it into a business."[33]

Those words hold a lot of truth in them. On the one hand, the fact that business principles are being applied to help accelerate the expansion of the Church of Jesus is a good thing. There is no need for church starters to get bogged down in reinventing the wheel for things like portable containers for portable churches, website designs, accounting services, people management software, strategic planning meetings, etc. All these and more are available from a variety of companies at an affordable price.

---

33   https://www.christianitytoday.com/edstetzer/2018/september/thoughts-on-church-planting-industry-capacity-ed-stetzer.html

That's good for church leaders and the businesses that are supporting them.

But the business side of being the church becomes a problem when the actual ministry of the Church is conducted as a business. When parishioners become customers, strategies for increasing the return on investment (R.O.I.) from each person in the pew become the priority, and ministry focus is determined by profitability (or not), then something is off. Literally by definition, a business exists to make a profit and a business that is not making a profit has no future. Churches exist to make disciples. Disciples are people, not products, and when we get confused about that, the organization we are leading may be wonderful in many ways, but it will not be the Church.

Tangling up business principles with disciple-making processes is perilous because we quickly find our foundation of faith shifting from Jesus in our heart to money in our bank. It's way too easy to go through spiritual motions that look and sound like faith on the surface but are actually based on the net worth of our accumulated assets.

The 20th-century church as a whole drifted seriously close to being guided by business principles first and ministry principles second. Routinely, the annual budgeting process started with "How much do we have?" followed by "What then will we do?" For many churches, this approach actually became the definition of good stewardship. On the surface, it does indeed sound reasonable. But this approach will not suffice in the 21st century.

The 21st-century approach will start with the question "What is God calling us to do?" and then look at the question "How will God resource what He is calling us to do?" Leading the church in this manner will require us to reactivate Spirit dependence. In order to know what God is calling us to do, we will need to be intentional about staying close to Him. We will need to shift our sense of security from the balance of our bank accounts and spreadsheets to the clarion call of hearing the still, small voice. We will need to be intentional about cultivating a determined closeness to God's Spirit that allows us to routinely hear his guidance, follow his promptings, and know what to do. Staying close to Jesus and doing what He says will lead us to a very different place than reading the latest book on church growth and doing what it says.

Business principles guide us toward safety and security. Following the path of Jesus will take us into the wilderness, cause us to run toward the danger, and incite us to act in ways that defy business logic. This posture of Spirit dependence is essential for fruitful ministry in the 21st century.

But, just how is Spirit dependence cultivated? Some might think that Spirit dependence begins with practicing the spiritual disciplines—pray, study of the Word, meditation, journaling, solitude, etc. But authentic Spirit dependence actually begins with a determination to be with Jesus on His Mission. Because he will always be guiding us to a place beyond our personal comfort zone, he will take us to risky, dangerous places where we will find ourselves desperate for Spirit empowerment. Ironically, stepping out onto mission with Jesus increases our awareness of our need for Spirit empowerment far more than the dutiful repetition of spiritual disciplines ever will.

I discovered this when I transitioned from my post as the founding director of Church Multiplication Network. Living in Springfield, Missouri, meant that the vast majority of my neighbors were professing Christians. The office I went to daily when I was in town required employees to demonstrate a commitment to following Jesus. The conferences and meetings I attended and spoke at were made up of Christian leaders who, hopefully, were committed followers of Jesus. Except for the person next to me on the plane wearing the ginormous headset that screamed "I want to be left alone," I lived in a segregated Christian bubble. Nevertheless, mostly every day, I spent time in prayer, reading the Word, occasionally journaling, practicing solitude, meditating on scripture, etc. I practiced these disciplines because I knew they were important to my personal discipleship and, honestly, because I encouraged others to do so and I did not want to be a hypocrite. When I think back on my practice of the presence of God during my time in the Christian bubble, it was something I did out of duty more than out of necessity.

When Cherri and I left Springfield to catalyze Urban Islands Project, everything changed dramatically. We went from knowing only people who professed faith in Jesus to knowing only people whose spiritual journeys were all over the spirituality spectrum. Some of our new friends identified as atheists. Others just considered themselves to be spiritual. Still others would best be described as anti-spirituality, considering any form of faith in a spiritual realm to actually be dangerous. Suddenly, we found ourselves in conversations where our human intellect was inadequate and our need to depend on the wisdom of the Spirit became a daily reality. My practice of the spiritual disciplines shifted from doing them out of a sense of duty to drawing close to God out of desperate necessity.

Looking back at the dominant priorities of the 20th-century church, one of the highly valued priorities was developing Christian safe spaces where believers could escape from the corruption of the world. This priority manifested itself in church calendars that were so packed with Bible studies, life groups, and worship gatherings that the only time believers ever needed to cross paths with the lost was when they were at work, school, or other public spaces where faith-sharing was discouraged at the very least and perhaps even prohibited.

This 20th-century form of hothouse Christianity had all sorts of unintended impacts on the missional effectiveness of the church. Perhaps the most serious was that it tended to isolate the people of the Church from the lost who desperately need the message of the church. Inside the carefully crafted walls of the Christian bubble, the message was loud and clear. But the philosophy of staying separate from the world prevented the message from getting outside the walls. When the message did leak out, too often it was in the form of angry-sounding rants against the evil practices of the missing—calling on people who have not surrendered to Christ to change their behavior to reflect Kingdom standards so that the whole world could look like it does inside the Christian bubble. This un-incarnated approach was not received well.

On a ministry trip to Oakland, California, I saw this cartoon by Joel Pett printed in the opinion page of the *East Bay Times*.

This characterization of the evangelical church is at least partially the result of the 20th-century segregated approach to being the Church. This is what happens when the Gospel message is lobbed over the walls of the safe Christian havens into the evil world out there. We have, albeit with good intentions, created this unfortunate reality. It will not serve us well as we seek to be on mission with Jesus in the 21st century.

The approach of the 21st-century church must be modified to reflect the fact that the purpose of Spirit dependence and empowerment is to equip the Church to incarnate the life-giving Gospel message into every nook and cranny of culture. Jesus made this promise to his disciples: "But you will receive power when the Holy Spirit comes on you; and you will be my witnesses in Jerusalem, and in all Judea and Samaria, and to the ends of the earth."[34] Jesus also indicated that the Church He is building would be irresistible to the "gates of Hell." His intention for the Church

---

34   Acts 1:8 NIV

He is building was never for it to be crouched safely behind ecclesiastical walls. The picture portrayed throughout scripture is a Church out in the danger actively engaged with the mission of seeking the missing. He has called us to be "out there" not safely "in here." And his promise is that as we act as witnesses, we will be empowered to be effective. The purpose of the empowerment is to enable us to thrive in the danger. We are equipped to have difficult and uncomfortable conversations with people who oppose the Gospel message because they've heard it only through a disembodied tweet on Twitter or sound bite on the evening news. Through the Spirit we have everything we need to have redemptive, spiritual conversations with our family, friends, neighbors, co-workers, classmates, etc.

The purpose of Spirit dependence is to enable us to be effectively on mission with Jesus. When Spirit dependence is reduced to a pious practice performed behind closed doors, we are missing the point. We've been called and equipped to go out into the chaos to live out and speak out the Gospel in the presence of the missing.

How do we cultivate spiritual dependence in life and for the organizations we lead?

1. The basic equation for successful spiritual leadership is one part strategy and one part miracle. You do and God does. Notice that Spirit dependence does NOT mean that we abandon our role in what God is doing. Paul says that "...we are co-workers in God's service; you are God's field, God's building."[35] We do what God guides and He does what we cannot do. Our part is strategy. His part is miracle. A miracle is not a strategy. We cannot say that we are just going to leave it all up to God and claim that we are depending on the Spirit. Walking

---

35   1 Corinthians 3:9

in Spirit means we will be walking. On the other hand, we must not place our trust in our strategic plans alone. If we do, we will quickly find ourselves on our own, building our own thing, apart from the Church that Jesus is building.

2. Spiritual warfare is real. The strategy side of the equation must include intentional and systematic spiritual warfare. The reality of the spiritual realm must never be taken for granted or ignored. We must cry out to God and trust that He is acting in the heavenlies to bind and loose, tearing down Satanic strongholds. In the 10th chapter of the Book of Daniel, the curtains are pulled back to allow us a glimpse of how spiritual warfare is conducted. "Then he continued, 'Do not be afraid, Daniel. Since the first day that you set your mind to gain understanding and to humble yourself before your God, your words were heard, and I have come in response to them. But the prince of the Persian kingdom resisted me twenty-one days. Then Michael, one of the chief princes, came to help me, because I was detained there with the king of Persia. Now I have come to explain to you what will happen to your people in the future, for the vision concerns a time yet to come.'"[36] From Daniel's perspective, his prayer efforts appeared to be fruitless, but tangible things were happening in the spirit realm. Spirit dependence means we cry out to God to do what we cannot do.

3. Another aspect of spirit dependence is praying to stay. Staying is an often-overlooked key to successfully being with Jesus on His Mission. Connections and relationships formed with missing people often take time to turn into decisions to follow Jesus. The adage says, "The

---

36   Daniel 10:12-14

grass looks greener on the other side," and all too often, Christian leaders move on before their work is truly complete. Of course, it is also possible to stay too long, but this is usually due to comfort. Quite often, the most difficult days of ministry happen just before the breakthrough comes. Spirit dependence means we trust that God will see us through the hard times and we can trust Him to bring the breakthrough in His time and His way.

4. The Sabbath is sacred. 20th-century leaders struggled with the Sabbath. Somehow, 20th-century leaders seemed to equate busy-ness with holiness. To be able to stand strong through the rigors of 21st-century culture, 21st-century leaders will need to take the Sabbath concept seriously, or they will not make it. We are already seeing a severe uptick in the number of driven leaders taking their own lives or disqualifying themselves from spiritual leadership through choices driven by self-reliance. Spirit dependence means we understand this is God's work and it will be just fine if we take a break! This truth became real to me in the process of starting my first church. After seven years of "shoulder to the grindstone" hard work, I decided to take a "Sabbatical." I was worried that the church would fall apart without my leadership. I chose to take my Sabbatical during the summer when attendance would be low anyway and planned to return at the end of the summer just in time to ride the wave of momentum into the fall. After several weeks, with fear and trepida-tion, fully expecting the numbers to be disastrous, I checked in to see how things were going. I was shocked to find out that during my absence, the church had experienced the highest attendance EVER. I

think God chuckled at my insecurities and gently reminded me that this was His Church, not mine. I was able to enjoy the rest of my Sabbatical due to a lesson learned that I will never forget.

5. Love your spouse. If you are married or plan to be married at some future date, it is crucial to keep in mind that a significant key to Spirit dependence is actively loving the person to whom you are married. Peter introduces the idea that broken spousal relationships can actually hinder prayers when he writes: "Husbands, in the same way be considerate as you live with your wives, and treat them with respect as the weaker partner and as heirs with you of the gracious gift of life, so that nothing will hinder your prayers."37

6. Trust and obey. Spiritual dependence is forged in the context of a lifestyle of absolute trust in Jesus and obedience to His guidance. Easy to say. Hard to do. Trusting and obeying are not one-time decisions that are made and moved on from. Trusting and obeying are habits that are lived out through the micro-decisions that are made over and over again in the moment. Will I trust Jesus right now or trust in my own instincts? Will I do what He says or take the path of least resistance? Will I simply mimic the leadership actions of my ministry hero or will I pursue Jesus and do what He says?

Reactivating spiritual dependence is crucial for the long haul of missional effectiveness. Spiritual dependence is born on our knees but matures as we walk out into the fray. In the fray, we quickly arrive at the end of ourselves and are aware of our dependence on the presence and power of God. Yes, the Denver Seven leaders needed to pray, but for their spiritual dependence to truly be activated, they needed to go to the coffee shop.

---

37   1 Peter 3:7

IN THEIR OWN WORDS...

A story of reactivating Spirit dependence.

Kurtis and Sarah Parks, founding pastors of Bridges, Nashville.

"I grew up in a pastor's home. I always had a love for music and started leading worship when I was 13. When I was old enough to do so, I continued leading worship while organizing rock bands that played in the bars and clubs. For a while, I had one foot in each world. One day, I felt like I needed to choose which way to go. I asked myself, 'Do I want to lead worship or do I want to be famous?' I decided to try the fame route.

"I decided to audition for *American Idol* and ended up making it to the top 50 that season. This little piece of fame fueled an unquenchable thirst to make it in the music industry. I started a band, moved to Nashville, and began touring the country in 2005. I felt like my sweet spot in performing was in bars and clubs, places Pastor Mark Batterson calls 'post-modern wells.' I learned to be at home at those 'wells.' Over time, the glamour wore off and by 2009, I found myself in kind of a rut playing the same clubs, same songs. I was doing everything I knew to do to make it big. Then it seemed that all my dreams were finally coming true.

"I got a call from the producer of another very-well-known live TV competition show. They had seen a video of me performing and offered to put my band straight to the show's top 10 contestants, without an audition! It seemed like a sure thing and the payoff for all my hard work. But on the call with the producer to finalize the deal, I felt the Holy Spirit leading me to turn down the offer. In obedience to that prompting of the Spirit, I turned down the deal and began to feel my unquenchable thirst for music fame being replaced with an unquenchable thirst to lead people in worship.

"I started leading worship again at a church in Nashville. Doors began to open for me to tour as a worship leader. One of the churches I was a guest worship leader at was National Community Church where Mark Batterson is pastor. Fell in love with the church and the city. Less than a year later, I joined the staff and became a worship leader, then a full-time campus pastor, and ended up overseeing the worship for all the NCC campuses.

"After some fantastic years on the staff of NCC, Sarah and I sensed the Spirit leading us to move to Nashville and start a new faith community. We moved to Nashville with a lot of pre-existing relationships who all said they want to be part of the new church, but only two of them actually followed through on that. That was hard. Building a team, finding a venue. Re-learning Nashville, which had become one of the fastest-growing cities since we'd moved away. Learning how to go from being a worship only-focused minister to the pastor/church planter role. I realized I needed to learn how to care for people, not just songs. I had a desire to help not only myself but the people in Nashville to understand that music is not the end-all be-all. In the early days of the planting process, the Spirit said to me, "I'm going to bring you the sons of David." That's what happened. Bridges Nashville is home to a lot of the "sons of David." In fact, the county our church meets in is Davidson County. The start-up process was really just discovering who would take the journey with us.

"Through a series of miracles, we ended up finding a place to meet at the Listening Room Cafe, one of the premier live music venues in Nashville. It's right in the center of a rapidly growing business district near the heart of downtown. We slowly pieced together a team and then slowly discovered who we would be. Since many of us are musicians, the pattern of our weekly gatherings needed to reflect that. We call it a *liturgy of music.* We teach through songs, with moments of testimony and scripture during worship. We write original music and use it to teach the Gospel. We do a "selah" break in the middle of the service where we play instrumental music and give people space to reflect, meditate, and pray. The format of all of our messages is inspired by Ted Talks, but the content comes straight out of scripture.

"It took a while for us to find our balance. The first six months after we began holding weekly services, our goal was simply to suck a little bit less every week. Over time, Bridges has developed into an amazing church made up of a lot of younger people. About 50 percent of us are college age. 70 percent are younger than 30.

"But the weekly service is only part of the Bridges story. Through praying and fasting, we discovered a calling to see Acts back in America. We read about the house church movement in China. We were inspired by Francis Chan's book *Letters to the Church.* Very early on, after our first Christmas service, we said we'd do church at home. One of our prayer leaders got 15 people together in his home, led a few songs in worship, shared the message via YouTube, prayed together, and did lunch together. He posted a picture on social media that I saw. I knew that THIS was the Acts Church! I spent 10 days praying and fasting at the top of the next year, and during that time, the Holy Spirit dumped downloads of ideas about how to do house church. We raised up house church leaders and empowered them. When COVID hit, we just pivoted to total house church supported by online services, Worship Nights, and Zoom Bible studies. Before COVID, we did house church about once a season—four or five times a year. Now we are doing house church all the time and plan to continue house churches at least once a month after COVID subsides, with a major emphasis on online church!

"In retrospect, I've realized that my conversation with the TV producer was a huge shift for me. In that moment, I recognized that I had been doing all the right things to become famous, but nothing clicked. Ironically, when the door to fame actually opened, it helped me see that if the Holy Spirit isn't in it, it's not worth doing. Turning my back on fame and deciding to follow the Spirit wherever he leads was a huge shift for me.

"Every day I try to start off praying in the spirit at least a half an hour out on my back deck. It's my prayer spot. Worship and prayer are like peanut butter and jelly. When I'm worshipping, I'm praying. I believe worship is prayer put to melody. In the process of starting a new church, you can read all the blogs and do all the things the experts say to do, but it wasn't until I came to the Lord and said "help" that I started to see the way forward. Strip away all the accolades, and God invites you to come just as you are. The interesting thing is that after I turned the producer down and moved to DC to make worship my focus, I started getting calls from major labels to use my songs. From this I learned, 'Don't seek opportunity. Seek God.' When you're seeking God, opportunity will find you. Crazy favor will come after you when you stop seeking it. Matt. 6:33. Just do that. Psalm 37:23. If he's ordering your steps, everything will be good.

"Two really important things I've learned through the process of starting this church:

"Number one—Planting a church is like parenting. One book will tell you nurture. Another will tell you nature. Follow the leading of the Holy Spirit, not a formula, as he's leading you to plant. I could not have strategized how this would play out. Let God define your story and vision. We've had people who've literally offered us tons of funding, but only if we did church their way. So, we turned them down, because God had put something specific on our hearts. You've got to do it in your own style. My personality is embedded in Bridges. That's OK God works through people, and personalities.

"Number two—If you always do what you've always done, you'll always be what you've always been. COVID has forced the hand of change. Take the risk. Don't be afraid to go against the flow. Every great change agent first looked like an idiot to those around them. Then books were written about their lives. Don't be afraid to look like an idiot."

Conclusion: A thousand ways to be right. An optimistic vision for the 21st-Century Church.

When I started my urban journey, I thought it was all about increasing the presence of the Church in the city. But on the way to increase the presence of the Church in the city, I realized that we had discovered an even bigger answer to an even bigger challenge. One day, I heard myself telling someone that I believe "God is bringing His Church back to the city to save Her Mission." Then COVID-19 disrupted everything. The future arrived sooner than anyone could have imagined. Ready or not, the culture of the 20th century is behind us and the 21st-century culture is now our new normal.

The Church has been content to hang on tightly to the strategies that served it well in the 20th century. As a result, the Church has become less and less effective with each passing day. Without intervention, the Church has been on a trajectory toward being completely out of step with Jesus and His Mission. The COVID-19 crisis provided the opportunity to hit the reset button, evaluate how faithfully we have been with Jesus on His Mission and decide to make the necessary shift. Some made the shift. Others paused and then settled back to the comfortable known ways of being the Church.

This book is a manifesto for intervention. We cannot afford to simply continue making small tweaks to our 20th-century template and hope for the desired missional results. It's time for an alarm to be sounded, for the church to wake up from a sheltered place of contentment and for strong, intentional actions to be taken.

The great news is that Jesus is building His Church, and we know that in the end, His Kingdom will prevail. We are not choosing whether or not His Church will weather the storm. Our choice is will we continue to be co-laborers with Him or not? We must know, if we choose His way, he will lead us into the danger to go after the missing. As we rush out in obedience to his call, there will certainly be times when we will wonder if we're in the right place, doing the right things for the right reasons. But He will be there right by our side, giving us His power to overcome whatever obstacles the enemy puts in our path.

The best days of the Church in America are in the future, not the past. I envision a day in the not-too-distant future when the new normal will emerge, bringing with it an irresistible wave of disciples making disciples who make disciples. The 20th-century noses and nickels question will be replaced with "Tell me about the disciples being made through your local expression of the Church." I see mega-churches strategically activating hundreds of sustainable micro-churches that will contextually proclaim the Gospel into every nook and cranny of culture. I see church organizations in cities complementing each other and thereby amplifying the redemptive voice of the Church in the greater culture. I see committed disciples skillfully injecting the Kingdom perspective into the crucible where culture is being created.

I hope that you will use this book as a catalyst for discovering the way forward for the church you are starting or leading. I hope you will wrestle with these shifts and make the changes that you need to make to be faithfully on mission with Jesus in the cultural context of the 21st century. I hope you'll lean on Jesus with all your heart, soul, mind, and strength. I hope you stop doing some things and start doing other things that will open new vistas of missional opportunity and joy for you and the church you lead. I'm hopeful that the story of the 21st-century church will play out much like the story of the 1st-century church—a church that, in spite of overwhelming cultural challenges, prevailed to set in motion a Jesus movement that, to this day, continues to gain momentum globally. Let it be so, Lord Jesus!

APPENDIX A

WHAT IS URBAN?

Discovering how to be the 21st-Century Church best begins where the story of man is going to end—in the city. The most important story of the 21st century is the emergence of the city as the crucible of culture and influence. For most of the history of people on this planet, we have lived in small towns and villages, rarely traveling far from the place of our birth. The emerging urban ubiquity is a relatively new development. In fact, as recently as 1905, 95 percent of the population of the world lived in rural communities. As we approach 2020, over 50 percent of humanity lives in an urban context, and all signs indicate that percentage is only going to increase in the years and decades to come. As Tim Keller has observed, our story begins in a garden, but it concludes in a city.[38]

On the one hand, cities are nothing new. Most historians have concluded that the earliest cities formed in what is now the Middle East. Basta and

---

38   https://www.cru.org/content/dam/cru/legacy/2012/02/A_Theology_of_Cities.pdf

Jericho were two of the earliest large settlements, both with populations of less than 2,000. Uruk is commonly believed to be the first named city. It was likely formed around 4000 B.C. when some scattered agriculturally based villages responded to drought by coming together near the Euphrates. It thrived over several millennia, reaching its peak population of perhaps 80,000 around 2900 B.C., making it the largest city in the world at the time.[39]

The first city with more than 100,000 inhabitants was possibly the Egyptian city of Avaris in approximately 1650 B.C. Babylon broke the 200,000 barrier in 600 B.C., and Alexandria may have become the first city with a population of over 1,000,000 in 100 B.C. The population of Rome peaked out at about 1,200,000 in 200 A.D. Hangzhou, China, became a city of 1,500,000 in 1300 A.D. In 1841, the population of London exceeded 1,900,000, and by 1900, London was the largest city in the world with a population of 6,500,000. London was displaced by New York City in 1925 when the Big Apple became home to 7,774,000. The population of Tokyo exceeded NYC in 1975 when it topped 15,000,000 and went on to become a city of 26,400,000 by the year 2000.[40]

As of this writing, Tokyo is now the seventh-largest city in the world, having been displaced by Chongqing, China, a city of 30,165,500 souls.41 The UN projects that by 2050, 68 percent of the world population will live in urban areas.42 Projected 2050 city populations are stunning: Mumbai, India, 42,403,631; Delhi, India, 36,156,789; Dhaka, Bangladesh, 35,193,184; Kinshasa, Democratic Republic of the Congo, 35,000,361. By 2050, over 50 cities in the world will each be home to a population of more than 10,000,000.[43]

39   https://en.m.wikipedia.org/wiki/Uruk
40   https://en.m.wikipedia.org/wiki/List_of_largest_cities_throughout_history
41   https://en.m.wikipedia.org/wiki/List_of_cities_proper_by_population
42   https://www.un.org/development/desa/en/news/population/2018-revision-of-world-urbanization-prospects.html
43   https://sites.uoit.ca/sustainabilitytoday/urban-and-energy-systems/Worlds-largest-cities/population-projections/city-population-2050.php

The world in 2050 would be unrecognizable to the Apostle Paul and other early church leaders. In Paul's day, the population of the ENTIRE world may have been about 200 million.[44] The largest cities at the time would have had 1 million people, but the vast majority (perhaps 97 percent) lived in rural towns and villages. It took over a thousand years for the world population to exceed 400 million and the rural/urban ratio remained about the same. By the year 1800, the number of residents on Planet Earth may have surpassed the 1 billion mark for the first time, but the ratio of urban to rural remained steady at about 3 percent.[45] By 2050, world population is projected to be over 9 billion, with only 32 percent living in rural contexts. It's clear that in the very near future, the vast majority of us will live in cities.

While it's true that cities have been around since the earliest days of humankind on this planet, cities as we know them today are a new sociological reality that has never been seen before. Over most of the course of history, perhaps 6,000 years, cities with more than 1 million inhabitants were rare and most people did not live in them. The dominant culture was rural, agrarian, and simple. For 6,000 years, rural settings provided the primary cultural context that shaped the forms and habits of the local church.

Why should we care about this? Because over the past 150 years, the place where the dominant culture is formed has dramatically shifted from rural to urban. Without going anywhere, the nature of the world around us has transported us to a completely different sociological and missiological reality than we've ever known before. Because sociology is an important factor in shaping our missiology, it is crucial that the people of the Church pay attention to what is happening around us. We must understand that this urban reality is unlike anything the world has ever seen before. New

---

44   https://www.census.gov/data/tables/time-series/demo/international-programs/historical-est-worldpop.html
45   ibid

sociological realities are demanding innovative missiological approaches. At least they should be.

On the surface, it looks like we are responding. Dry, tradition-infused worship gatherings have given way to energetic fog-and-light shows. Mega-cities have their mega-churches. Christian contemporary music has morphed into a plethora of music forms that convey the old, old story in every imaginable music style. Relevance and excellence have replaced habits and rituals as the foundations of missional effectiveness. "Church planting" is now a main focus of almost every Christian denomination and network.

But a look below the glittering surface is alarming. All but a few of the major denominations and networks are losing missional ground. Many are closing more churches than they are opening. They are gathering fewer people than they were the year before. The percentage of the population that identify as "Nones" is on the rise at an unprecedented pace. The number of churches relative to population in core urban communities is slipping. Urban church buildings are being sold to the highest bidder and turned into bars, event centers, condominiums, etc. According to David Olson's research, the actual number of church attendees in America stayed about the same (53 million) from 1990 to 2006, while the American population increased by about 53 million. Yes, it's the same number and it means the percentage of Americans attending church dropped over that 16-year period.[46]

It's not a coincidence that the current crisis of the Church has paralleled the mega-trend toward urban culture. We have seen that the history of cities was relatively static for thousands of years. But the past 150 years have amounted to an urban revolution. Here's an admittedly over-simplistic summary of the recent history of the city:

46   The American Church in Crisis, David Olson, 2006.

- Modern cities formed in the 1800s when the economy transitioned from being based on agriculture to a manufacturing economy.
- Manufacturing plants were built near each other close to small cities with a good base of potential employees.
- Big manufacturers built affordable housing near their plants and formerly rural people migrated to cities for jobs.
- This rapid population increase turned small towns into big cities that lacked adequate infrastructure to support the burgeoning population.
- Pollution, crime, grit, and grime became the main characteristics of the stereotypical cities.
- The economy began to shift from manufacturing toward an information economy.
- Jobs and suburbs sprang up on the outskirts of the cities. People followed. Churches followed the people.
- Cities experienced negative population growth.
- Land values fell.
- Developers stepped in and snatched up the cheap city land.
- They redeveloped cities into desirable places to live and work and play.
- People moved back in.
- The Church has tried to follow but with few exceptions has not thrived.

As a result, city centers have become virtual "church deserts" inhabited by masses of humanity with little or no connection to a worshipping community. In general, as the density of the population goes up, the presence of the Church goes down. This should not be!

In his book, *The Great Evangelical Recession: 6 Factors That Will Crash The American Church... and How To Prepare*, pastor, author, and award-winning journalist John S. Dickerson writes, "Very few of us live in New York, Los Angeles, Washington DC, or Silicon Valley. Few of us work in public universities or at mainstream media outlets. However, the majority of influential culture shapers in our age do live and work in these areas. As such, we are out of touch with the mindset, worldview, and values of the relative few who frame the debates, shape the policies, and name the assumptions for America's developing generations. I know these are simplistic, broad strokes. The point is that few of us will realize how quickly culture has changed until that change bleeds in from the coastal metropolises to the middle-American cities, comfortable suburbs, and insulated social circles we call home."[47] Dickerson clearly identifies one of the greatest challenges of the Church. The Church is not where the shapers of a culture are. Research indicates that the vast majority of people who choose to follow Christ, do so because of a personal connection to a devoted follower of Christ. It's tough to build a relationship with someone if you are never around them.

This does not bode well for the urban future we are hurtling toward. The future is more urban, not less. And the culture that is being exported from the urban crucible of cultural formation is not that of the Church. To effectively be on mission with Jesus in the 21st century, we are going to need to change our habits or we will be guilty of the definition of insanity—doing the same thing over and over again and hoping for different results. But what will we do? Because modern cities present a challenge we've never faced before, we can no longer rely on past strategies to guide us. How will we overcome this previously unseen threat to our missional effectiveness?

47   The Great Evangelical Recession, John S. Dickerson, Baker Books, January 2013.

A part of discovering the answer to that question starts with a good working definition of "urban." What comes to mind when you say or hear the word "urban"? If every reader of this book was able to respond in real time to that question, the answers would likely all be different. When a challenge is hard to define, the solution will be hard to discover. Therefore, in order to create a missional strategy to address the urban challenge, we must pause to define what we mean by "urban."

One way to begin to understand urban is to contrast urban with suburban. A working paper by Whitney Airgood-Obrycki and Shannon Rieger of Harvard's Joint Center for Housing Studies is helpful in seeing the contrast between urban and suburban.[48] Here is a brief summary of their findings.

- Most Americans live in suburbs. According to research by the Pew Research Center, the breakdown is 55 percent suburban, 31 percent urban, and 14 percent rural.[49]

- The vast majority of suburbanites own single-family homes. In the suburbs, 75 percent are homeowners of single-family homes, compared with about 40 percent in urban neighborhoods.

- Urbanites are more likely to use other forms of transportation besides a car. Ninety percent of suburbanites commute by car, compared to 75 percent of urbanites.

- Urban neighborhoods have more people per square mile than suburbs. Suburbs contain about 1,900 people per square mile compared to an average of about 6,500 per square mile in a typical urban community.

48 https://www.citylab.com/life/2019/06/suburbs-definition-census-data-way-of-life/591343/?utm_campaign=citylab-daily-newsletter&utm_medium=email&silve-rid=%25%25RECIPIENT_ID%25%25&utm_source=newsletter
49 https://www.pewsocialtrends.org/2018/05/22/demographic-and-economic-trends-in-urban-suburban-and-rural-communities/

- Despite the forces of gentrification at play in many urban communities, the poverty rate is higher in urban neighborhoods—about twice that of suburban poverty rates.
- Suburbs are overwhelmingly white compared to urban neighborhoods that tend to be about 50 percent white.

With these facts in mind, a general definition of urban would include some of the following distinguishing characteristics:

- Multi-family living spaces. More than half of urban residents live in multi-family dwellings (apartments, condos, townhomes, etc.).
- More diverse transportation. Urbanites are less dependent on automobiles.
- More population density. Urban neighborhoods average about three times as many people per square mile as the average suburban density.
- Lower average incomes. Despite the growing realities of gentrification, urban incomes tend to be lower than suburban incomes and poverty rates tend to be higher.
- More diverse. Urban neighborhoods are more ethnically diverse.

However, *urban* is more than just average incomes, densities, and diversity. A key reality that differentiates urban from suburban is diversity in proximity. Cities are like a thousand small towns or islands in close proximity to each other. It is this reality that led us to name the project we lead "Urban Islands Project." Proximity is key to understanding the foundational reality that makes urban, well, urban.

For example, I live in a Denver neighborhood known to locals as Uptown. This neighborhood is one of the oldest residential neighborhoods in Denver. In the early days, the most common housing options were very large single-family dwellings. Over the years, many of those single-family homes have been replaced with mid- and high-rise multi-family apartments and condo buildings, resulting in a quirky, eclectic mix of old and new, high and low, pricey and affordable places to live interspersed with offices, restaurants, shops, banks, and other retail services. The neighborhood just to the south of Uptown is called Capitol Hill, likely due to the fact that it sits just east of the state capitol building. Cap Hill is more residential than Uptown, although it too is sprinkled with unique restaurants, offices, and small businesses. But Cap Hill has a different ethos than Uptown... it's tricky to put your finger on it, but having lived here for a while, it's as obvious to me as the nose on my face. These are just two of the 78 or so neighborhoods or islands that cluster together to make up the city known as Denver.

Each of these 78 neighborhoods is unique. Uniqueness in proximity is a defining characteristic that distinguishes urban from suburban and rural. Although suburbs certainly have their own unique characteristics, they tend to have a lot more in common than proximate urban neighborhoods do. The strong identity of neighborhoods is the basis for street gangs claiming their territory. Urban residents tend to be highly aware of and take pride in their neighborhood. When Josh Perkins played on the Gonzaga Bulldogs basketball team that made it to the NCAA Division I Final Four in 2017, he listed his hometown as Park Hill, Colorado. Park Hill is a neighborhood in Denver, not a town. But Josh identified more with his hood than with his city. So part of the definition of urban is a strong association with a place that is in close proximity to places with their own distinct identity.

Another factor to consider in our definition of urban is the phenomenon known as *multi-nucleation*. The core neighborhood of a large city is often referred to as the Central Business District or CBD. These core neighborhoods are where the tallest buildings are built and residential density is highest due to the existence of vertical neighborhoods (high-rise apartment and condo buildings). The CBD is typically surrounded by first-ring neighborhoods where the buildings are tall, but shorter than the CBD buildings, and residential is more prevalent than in the CBD. The next ring of neighborhoods tends to be more residential and less business/retail oriented. Eventually, the city limits give way to first-ring suburbs where the homes tend to be larger and single-family and the population density tends to be lower.

If only it were that simple. Transportation lines tend to create multi-nucleation—meaning that developed cities rarely have only one CBD. Other smaller, but impactful CBDs emerge along transportation corridors—freeways, bus lines, and light rail/commuter train routes. When the economic conditions make sense, vertical neighborhoods spring up around the interchanges and train stops and along the bus lines that radiate out from the heart of the city

The result is that urban places can spring up far away from the main CBD of the city core. If you've ever visited Atlanta, Georgia, you've seen multi-nucleation in the form of junior CBDs surrounded by suburban subdivisions sprinkled around the sprawl of the metroplex.

At least one more characteristic that seems to go hand in hand with urban is a higher incidence of crime. But not necessarily a higher crime rate. The fact is that because urban centers tend to have more people per square mile, they will also have more knuckleheads per square mile. To paraphrase urban veteran Pastor Tim Keller, cities have more of everything. But that does not mean cities automatically have a higher rate of crime per capita. A 2019 article in *USA Today* listed the 25 most dangerous cities in the United States. Springfield, Missouri (population 167,000) is listed as the12th-most-dangerous city in the U.S. Denver (population 730,000) didn't make the top 25. I've lived in both and I can tell you that I've seen more evidence of crime in Denver. But that's because urban neighborhoods simply have more people doing life in proximity. More people = more good and more bad. I never saw a homeless person in my Springfield subdivision. In my Denver neighborhood, I encounter homeless people every day. I rarely heard a siren in Springfield. Sirens are a normal part of the background noise in Denver. Oddly enough, urban has a rough edge to it that makes it feel more crime infested than it really is.

There is one more crucial characteristic that differentiates urban from suburban and rural—urban is a culture, perhaps even a worldview. Urban culture is the crucible out of which big cultural trends are born. The fact that in general the Church has left the neighborhood has resulted in a spiritual vacuum in the heart of our cities.

What, then, is the definition of urban?

In view of the complex nature of the question, we may need to agree that there are at least two valid definitions of "urban.

The sociological definition:

A community or neighborhood geographically

- in or near a "Central Business District" or multi-nucleated hub,
- where the population density exceeds 3,000 people per square mile,
- the ethnicity of the residents is diverse,
- the housing options include a lot of multi-family units,
- at least 20 percent of the population commutes to work or play using a transportation mode that is not a car,

- the average income levels of nearby residents is diverse,
- crime is a concern.

It's also important to remember that this definition will be manifested in a variety of forms. Here's a non-exhaustive list of some of the different types of urban places I've observed:

- Vertical high cost
- Vertical economically challenged
- Single immigrant group focused
- Art district
- Multi-family millennial magnet apartment buildings
- Central business district high-rises
- Economically challenged and gentrifying
- Urban suburban neighborhoods
- Suburban urban neighborhoods
- Middle-city neighborhoods that have stagnated
- Event/recreation-oriented neighborhoods
- Historic, preserved neighborhoods
- Gang -run neighborhoods
- Gated neighborhoods

But urban also has a philosophical definition:

Urban is a worldview, birthed in the midst of large numbers of people living in proximity and exported to every sector of society. The urban worldview tends to be:

- Self-confident.
- Optimistic.
- Self-sufficient.

- Self-reliant.
- Agnostic.
- Secular.
- The dominant worldview of the 21st century.

With these definitions as our guides, we will now consider the challenges and opportunities that the trend toward urbanization presents to the Church.

APPENDIX B
WHY DOES GOD CARE ABOUT CITIES?

For this book to be a complete overview of how the Church that Jesus is building should be strategically present in cities, we need to look at the biblical record of God's concern for cities.

Why Cities Matter by Justin Buzzard and Stephen T. Um and Center Church by Tim Keller are excellent books that address this question more thoroughly than we will in these chapters. I hope you'll acquire those books to assist you in forming a robust theology of the city and why cities are so crucial to the Mission of God.

The purpose of this appendix is to point the reader to the strong evidence that God cares deeply for cities.

Let's begin with what may seem like a self-evident statement that summarizes God's love for cities succinctly. God loves people. Cities are home to dense populations of people. Therefore, God loves cities. You won't find these words anywhere in a single scripture passage, but the idea is a theme throughout the scriptural story of mankind, from beginning to end. "We begin in a garden, but end in a city." —Tim Keller

Adam and Eve—God was with them. Genesis 3:8 says that they heard God walking.

"Then the man and his wife heard the sound of the LORD God as he was walking in the garden in the cool of the day, and they hid from the LORD God among the trees of the garden." NIV

Abraham was looking for a city. Hebrews 11:10 "Abraham was confidently looking forward to a city with eternal foundations, a city designed and built by God."

God raised up cities—Cain had sexual relations with his wife, and she became pregnant and gave birth to Enoch. Then Cain founded a city, which he named Enoch, after his son. Genesis 4:17

God took down cities4 —Then they said, "Come, let's build a great city for ourselves with a tower that reaches into the sky. This will make us famous and keep us from being scattered all over the world."5 But the Lord came down to look at the city and the tower the people were building.6 "Look!" he said. "The people are united, and they all speak the same language. After this, nothing they set out to do will be impossible for them!7 Come, let's go down and confuse the people with different languages. Then they won't be able to understand each other." Genesis 11:4-7 NLT

Jonah and Nineveh—The entire book of Jonah is a clear indication of God's attitude toward cities. "Then the Lord said, 'You feel sorry about the plant, though you did nothing to put it there. It came quickly and died quickly. 11 But Nineveh has more than 120,000 people living in spiritual darkness, not to mention all the animals. Shouldn't I feel sorry for such a great city?'" Jonah 4:10-11 NLT

God commanded his people to work for the good of the city. Jeremiah 29: 4-7 "This is what the Lord of Heaven's Armies, the God of Israel, says to all the captives he has exiled to Babylon from Jerusalem: 5 'Build homes, and plan to stay. Plant gardens, and eat the food they produce. 6 Marry and have children. Then find spouses for them so that you may have many grandchildren. Multiply! Do not dwindle away! 7 And work for the peace and prosperity of the city where I sent you into exile. Pray to the Lord for it, for its welfare will determine your welfare.'"

This particular passage is particularly stunning. God is speaking through His prophet to His people, who have been taken captive by their enemies. Rather than promising deliverance or commanding disobedience, God clearly wants them to influence their captors by living vigorous lives in their midst.

Jesus grieved over Jerusalem. Luke 13:34-35 "O Jerusalem, Jerusalem, the city that kills the prophets and stones God's messengers! How often I have wanted to gather your children together as a hen protects her chicks beneath her wings, but you wouldn't let me. 35 And now, look, your house is abandoned. And you will never see me again until you say, 'Blessings on the one who comes in the name of the Lord!'"

Paul strategically started churches in cities. A good portion of the Book of Acts is an account of Paul moving from influential city to influential city.

The story of man ends up in a city.

Revelation 21 (NLT)—Then I saw a new heaven and a new earth, for the old heaven and the old earth had disappeared. And the sea was also gone. 2 And I saw the holy city, the new Jerusalem, coming down from God out of heaven like a bride beautifully dressed for her husband. 3 I heard a loud shout from the throne, saying, "Look, God's home is now among his people! He will live with them, and they will be his people. God himself will be with them. 4 He will wipe every tear from their eyes, and there will be no more death or sorrow or crying or pain. All these things are gone forever." 5 And the one sitting on the throne said, "Look, I am making everything new!" And then he said to me, "Write this down, for what I tell you is trustworthy and true." 6 And he also said, "It is finished! I am the Alpha and the Omega—the Beginning and the End. To all who are thirsty I will give freely from the springs of the water of life. 7 All who are victorious will inherit all these blessings, and I will be their God, and they will be my children. 8 "But cowards, unbelievers, the corrupt, murderers, the immoral, those who practice witchcraft, idol worshipers, and all liars—their fate is in the fiery lake of burning sulfur. This is the second death." 9 Then one of the seven angels who held the seven bowls containing the seven last plagues came and said to me, "Come with me! I will show you the bride, the wife of the Lamb." 10 So he took me in the Spirit to a great, high mountain, and he showed me the holy city, Jerusalem, descending out of heaven from God. 11 It shone with the glory of God and sparkled like a precious stone—like jasper as clear as crystal. 12 The city wall was broad and high, with twelve gates guarded by twelve angels. And the names of the twelve tribes of Israel were written on the gates. 13 There were three gates on each side—east, north, south, and west. 14 The wall of the city had twelve foundation stones, and on them were written the names of the twelve apostles of the Lamb. 15 The angel who talked to me held in his hand a gold measuring stick to measure the city, its gates, and its wall. 16 When he measured it, he found it was a square, as wide as it was long. In fact, its length and width and height were each 1,400 miles. 17 Then he measured the walls and found them to be 216 feet thick (according to the human standard used by the angel). 18 The wall was made of jasper, and the city was pure gold, as clear as glass. 19 The wall of the city was built on foundation stones inlaid with twelve precious stones: the first was jasper, the second sapphire, the third agate, the fourth emerald, 20 the fifth onyx, the sixth carnelian, the seventh chrysolite, the eighth beryl, the ninth topaz, the tenth chrysoprase, the eleventh jacinth, the twelfth amethyst. 21 The twelve gates were made of pearls—each gate from a single pearl! And the main street was pure gold, as clear as glass. 22 I saw no temple in the city, for the Lord God Almighty and the Lamb are its temple. 23 And the city has no need of sun or moon, for the glory of God illuminates the city, and the Lamb is its light. 24 The nations will walk in its light, and the kings of the world will enter the city in all their glory. 25 Its gates will never be closed at the end of day because there is no night there. 26 And all the nations will bring their glory and honor into the city. 27 Nothing evil will be allowed to enter, nor anyone who practices shameful idolatry and dishonesty—but only those whose names are written in the Lamb's Book of Life.

APPENDIX C
COMPLEXITY—THE URBAN CHALLENGE

For most of my life, despite a brief taste of dwelling in a rural town, I've lived in communities that are best described as "suburban." Five years ago, my wife and I made the decision to move into a city neighborhood called Uptown in the heart of Denver, which is a mid-sized American city with a city population of 730,000 and a metro population of about 3 million, making it the 19th-largest city and metro in the United States. So, while Denver is definitely not New York City (NYC is really in a class by itself), it contains the full spectrum of the urban experience. Our Uptown neighborhood is one square mile and home to about 14,000 residents (and growing).[50]

Our experience of moving from a deep familiarity with suburban living to a direct and growing familiarity with urban living has been educational to say the least. We have quickly discovered that many of our assumptions

---

50   http://www.city-data.com/neighborhood/Uptown-Denver-CO.html

about cities and city living were either completely wrong or mildly skewed versions of the real thing. Perhaps our most important lesson has been that the urban context is a challenging place for the Church to thrive. Even more concerning, the Church seems content to remain unaware of the missional opportunity right under its nose. Every day, suburban churches are sending missions teams to needy nations around the world, driving right past the spiritual desert in their midst. The rare local churches that do recognize the missional opportunity back away from the daunting challenges they encounter in the urban context. In this appendix we will take a look at some of the challenges that the Church must find a way to overcome in order to thrive.

DIVERSITY

Most churches and church organizational headquarters are physically located in rural or suburban communities. This means that the majority of church and denominational leaders live and work in a rural or suburban community. Rural and suburban communities tend to be culturally homogeneous. Rural and suburban residents tend to look and sound the same. The homes they live in are similar. Suburban neighborhood designs tend to be uniform and feel almost universally similar. The suburban experience is very much like the experience of an indoor mall—if you've seen one, you've seen them all. In fact, once you are inside a mall, it's difficult to know where the mall is geographically located because they all have the same stores, layout, products, and general experience.

While cities do have some general similarities to each other (tall buildings, traffic, multi-family dwellings, etc.), city neighborhoods are characterized by a broad spectrum of extreme diversity. Ethnic diversity, lifestyle diversity, economic diversity—if suburbs tend to be where similar people live near each other, cities are places where very different people live in hyper-close proximity to each other.

Diversity tends to fall into six categories that the urban church must be mindful of—ethnic, lifestyle, economic, neighborhood ethos, transportation, and leisure pursuits.

Ethnic diversity is what usually jumps to mind when people hear the word "diversity." A high degree of ethnic diversity is a key differentiator between the urban and suburban experience. In general, cities have a much higher level of ethnic diversity than a typical suburb. Compounding the challenge is that urban diversity is typically uneven. Whereas suburban homogeneity is mostly even, urban diversity is itself diversified. Many urban neighborhoods are composed of people from a variety of ethnic backgrounds. Other neighborhoods are made up of immigrants from a common country. The common urban experience is that urban residents are more likely to interact with people from a different ethnic origin than are their suburban counterparts.

Lifestyle diversity has to do with the varieties of ways that people actually live their lives. Suburbia is generally made up of families composed of two parents and their children living in single-family homes. Suburban homogeneity is almost non-existent in urban neighborhoods. Neighborhoods in the urban core tend to have few children. Many single adults share space in multi-family living units. Gay and lesbian families are much more common in urban places. When urban neighborhoods become the home of a cluster of immigrants, it is not unusual for multi-generational families to be living in housing units intended for a single family made up of a mom, a dad, and a couple of kids.

Suburbs tend to be home to clusters of people of similar economic status. Some city neighborhoods are economically hyper-diverse—homeless, middle-class, very wealthy, and starving artists all sharing the sidewalks together. Other city neighborhoods tend to be very concentrated groupings of people who share an economic status. High-rise condo buildings tend to create very focused groupings of people who can afford to live in them.

Neighborhood ethos diversity. By neighborhood ethos, I mean the "feel" of a locality. Urban neighborhoods span an incredibly broad spectrum of "experience." From the aforementioned high-rise condo buildings, to the edgy vibe of the arts district, to the hard-scrabble challenged hoods, to the sleepy in-between neighborhoods, etc. Every neighborhood has its own unique personality, attributes, challenges, and opportunities.

Transportation diversity is a real thing created by how people get to work and play. When I lived in the suburbs and needed to go somewhere, I never considered any option except using my car. But as a city dweller, I typically go through six or seven transportation options before I decide how I will get where I'm going. Here are some actual options I consider every time I plan a trip. 1.) Walk. Because of where I live, I can walk to my dentist, my doctor, five different grocery stores, 168 different restaurants, two great parks, my dry cleaner, etc. 2.) Ride my bike. When my trip will take more than 20 minutes to walk, then my bike is a good option. 3.) Take a scooter. Biking may cause me to work up a sweat. When I'm going to a meeting where getting hot and sweaty would be a liability, electric scooters are a great, sweat-free alternative to the bike. 4.) Lyft/Uber/other ride-sharing services. For short trips where a bike or scooter isn't the best option and parking will be a problem, ride-sharing is the way to go. 5.)

Public bus options. Depending on the destination, riding a bus is sometimes a great, affordable option. 6.) Light or commuter rail. In my case, using commuter rail to get to the airport is more affordable, safer, and quicker than driving my car. 7.) Renting a car is sometimes a better option than driving my own car. 8.) Driving my own car is my last option. Needless to say, it's not uncommon for me to go for days without driving my car. Most of these alternative transportation options provide far more opportunities to interact with other people than using my car. Also, I rarely spend long periods of time stuck in traffic.

Leisure diversity. Leisure pursuits are diverse in the city. Public parks are huge and inviting. Bike lanes and trails criss-cross the urban core. Proximity to destinations like museums, art galleries, shopping, and restaurant options can be perks for many urban dwellers.

Diversity is a challenge for the Church because conformity has emerged as a high value for many churches. Too often, making conformity a core value has the unintended consequence of sending a message to people who are "different" that they are not welcome here. Churches often perceive themselves as "friendly and welcoming," but that feeling is not always shared by newcomers to the church. Some churches even pride themselves on being places where everyone looks and acts exactly the same. When a church serves in a homogeneous context, the challenge of conformity is not so obvious. But urban dwellers, who are accustomed to moving from one diverse context to another, find the homogenous conformity off-putting and strange.

ECONOMY

Another challenge for the Church in the urban context is the Economic Challenge. Some urban neighborhoods are made up of citizens who are economically challenged. Other urban neighborhoods are affordable only to people who are on the top end of the economic scale. The result is that typical local church budget assumptions simply do not apply for most urban churches.

For example, in most suburban communities, it is reasonable to expect that a church will be able to gather enough parishioners with adequate income to fund a sustainable budget. This is not a reasonable expectation in most urban situations. Churches in low-income communities are hobbled by the lack of income of their parishioners. High-end communities are hobbled by the high costs of rent and/or property. Right or wrong, many suburban church starters are guided by the 200 rule—start with 200 or more on launch day and in two to three years (at most) the church will be self-sustaining. For several reasons, it's difficult to apply this formula in the urban context. Finding a meeting space that will accommodate 200 people is a challenge. Most urban gathering places will accommodate about 100 or 20,000, with very few options in between. The mid-sized meeting spaces are rare and the costs are prohibitive. Some urban church planters in upscale neighborhoods face high costs for renting facilities that will never be able to hold enough tithe payers to cover the rental costs. The math just doesn't work. On the other end of the spectrum, lower-income neighborhoods struggle with maintaining a small income, so even if costs are lower (and there is no guarantee they will be), the income is not adequate to cover expenses. The result is that in general, urban churches have fewer people and higher costs. Unfortunately, the traditional church-starting and sustaining approaches simply don't apply.

SECULAR/SPIRITUAL WORLDVIEW

A glance at any map portraying the geography of politics will show cities as blue blobs surrounded by a red sea. Blue has become the color most commonly associated with a liberal worldview, and red typically denotes a conservative mindset. My experience living in both the blue blob and the red sea confirms that this is not just a stereotype. It's a reality. And it's a challenge for the Church.

Why? Because the Church, especially the Evangelical part of the Church, is viewed as mostly aligned with conservative political positions. As a result, on the surface, the Church is automatically handicapped in an urban cultural context. As one of my gay neighbors told me, "I can't go to church, because I'm gay." The blue blob reality is that the majority of urban dwellers are under the impression that the church does not want them and will not welcome them. My friend felt this way despite the fact that most urban churches identify themselves as "affirming."

Additionally, the secular worldview that dominates the urban mindset creates an underlying bias against the Church. Not only is the Church not welcoming, it's actually considered harmful. Really. The urban stereotype of religious people is that they are uneducated, prone to hypocrisy (recent sex abuse scandals in the Catholic and major Evangelical churches have not helped at all), opposed to science, and desire to impose unhelpful moral standards on everyone around them. *The Handmaid's Tale*, a popular program produced by the Hulu streaming service (Hulu's corporate head-quarters are in Los Angeles), seems to be a portrayal of what secularists think society would look like if the Church were in charge. It's an ugly portrayal—a scary police state run by Bible-quoting politicians who execute people for immoral acts by day and secretly participate in even more evil immoral acts by night. Dark depictions like this are more common than not in popular media and serve to reinforce the suspicions of secularized viewers. This dominating secular worldview means church starters and sustainers begin with a strategic and missional disadvantage that must be factored into ministry strategies.

But I labeled this challenge "secular/spiritual" for a reason. Juxtaposed up against a strong secular bent is an appreciation and respect for spirituality. Many urban residents find inspiration in the Bible and the Bhagavad Gita and the Koran and the Upanishads and even in visitations from dead relatives and pets. Christianity feels too confining to spiritual people who custom-build systems of spirituality out of any and all religious systems that resonate with them. Acknowledging this secular/spiritual stew is a great way to introduce our next challenge—religious diversity.

Religious diversity. The most popular church start-up strategies were formed in a suburban context. They are built on several assumptions that are generally true in the suburbs. Assumption one: Many people living in this community have some sort of history with the Christian Church and would be willing to attend a good, proactive Christian church if they were invited. Assumption two: It is possible to fairly quickly gather people with a basic understanding of Christian stewardship so that the financial needs of the church will be met. Assumption three: Affordable, accessible meeting space is readily available. Assumption four: Residents of this community have the ability to easily get themselves to church gatherings.

The problem is that NONE of these assumptions are accurate in most urban settings. The religious diversity in urban neighborhoods is similar to the ethnic diversity of urban neighborhoods—very diverse. All manner of religious backgrounds are represented. Most urban people don't have any familiarity with Christian stewardship. Meeting space is hard to come by. An increasing number of urbanites are choosing other means of transportation besides a car. The combination of all these factors means that traditional approaches to being the church struggle to survive in the urban context.

COMMUNITY

Having lived in homogeneous suburban neighborhoods for most of my life, I thought cities were just bigger versions of suburbs where most people were too busy to know their neighbors. The reality could not be further from the truth.

The average urban dweller is ensconced in a matrix of overlapping and siloed communities. First, they live in a neighborhood with a personality and spheres of relationships all its own. Then, they share common space with people they commute to work with—sidewalk, subway, bus, elevators, hallways, the barista at the coffee shop on the way, etc. They have their work network of friends, co-workers etc. After work is done, it's time to unwind at a bar, concert, party, meet-up, park, sports league. The variety of social opportunities available to urban people is broad and complicated. Urban dwellers often have five or six circles of relationship—some that overlap and others that don't. So they do know their neighbors. Sort of.

And yet, studies show that urban dwellers suffer from a nagging sense of loneliness. Fifty-five percent of Londoners claim to be lonely sometimes, despite being surrounded by millions of people. In Tokyo, some people actually "rent" friends just to have someone to talk with.[51] And so, ironically, urbanites tend to have many circles of connectivity and at the same time feel lonely. And they feel too busy to cram in anything else, like being part of a local church. In fact, for a person unfamiliar with what it means to be part of a faith community, joining a church just sounds like a lot of work that will not be worth the effort.

The urban context is a challenging and daunting place for the Church to exist. Head-spinning diversity, wallet-breaking economics, unfamiliar philosophies, and complicated community all add up to a wall of resistance that seems to be coated with some sort of "church repellant." Increasingly, the challenges of the urban culture will be the challenges that every community faces. And yet, along with these challenges come some missional opportunities for the church that we cannot afford to overlook. The opportunities of being the Church in the city will be the subject of our next appendix.

---

51   https://www.citymetric.com/horizons/
why-living-big-city-so-isolating-lonely-isolation-loneliness-4210

APPENDIX D
PROXIMITY—THE URBAN OPPORTUNITY

It's true that the urban context is a daunting challenge for the Church. However, urban contexts provide some very positive opportunities for the church that are currently being underutilized because the presence of the Church is too thin. In this appendix, we will explore the strategic benefits of being on mission with Jesus in the urban context.

INFLUENCE

Cities are gathering places for culture-shapers. In fact, cities tend to be where big cultural ideas are birthed, nurtured, and distributed out to the general culture. The Church has typically responded to this reality as a threat, because many of the big ideas and philosophical concepts emanating from cities are diametrically opposed to biblical truth. Naturally, spiritual leaders and people of faith feel a responsibility to defend the truth. Unfortunately, by the time the Church reacts, the un-Christian concepts have already made their way into public attitudes and policies. Restoring the presence of the Church in the city puts the people of the Church in proximity to culture-shapers and empowers the Church to influence public attitudes and policies when they are in their earliest stages of formation.

The idea that a church can actually influence culture flies in the face of business as usual for the modern church. Most ministry strategies are reactive or designed to lure spiritually needy people onto church turf so they can see and hear the truth. When we wait for un-Christian ideas to go mainstream in the culture, or we believe that the best place for truth to be engaged is in our carefully cultivated worship spaces, it's like an Olympic athlete who decides to give his opponents a two-second headstart in a 100-meter race. Why would anyone do that? We end up constantly playing catch-up. Meanwhile, un-Christian philosophies are running rampant in popular culture. Our kids are growing up in a world where Christians ideas are relegated to the sidelines. The only option left to us is to oppose everything, and too often we just sound like shrill and petty fun-suckers.

What if we decided to influence the culture where it is being born? That's the incredible opportunity of increasing the presence of the Church in the city. The voice of the Church can once again become part of the process of culture creation. If the Church is engaging directly with the cultural architects who are inventing the future, we may have the opportunity to embed biblical truth into the cultural ideas that are being formed and exported to the suburbs and rural communities.

Unhealthy secular ideas birthed in a spiritual vacuum are a legitimate concern for spiritual leaders everywhere. But our current strategy is passive and reactionary. Recognizing the opportunity to influence cultural formation with a strategy that is proactive and pre-emptive potentially gives the Church a headstart in the race to shape societal beliefs and attitudes.

RELATIONSHIP

I do realize the previous opportunity may sound a little idealistic. It's certainly fair to react to the optimistic idea of leveraging influence with the realistic "Yeah, but how?" question. The opportunity for the Church to have a seat at the table of inventing the future is very real, but it will require breaking some old habits and learning some new ones.

First, cities hold great potential for forming deep and meaningful relationships with your fellow city dwellers. This was one of the biggest surprises to me when I made the transition from being a lifelong suburbanite to living in an urban neighborhood. My stereotype of city dwellers was that they are all busy people who prefer to remain anonymous and suffer from a high degree of loneliness. That stereotype may indeed be true for some, but I've discovered an interesting reality of city life that actually makes urban neighborhoods MORE conducive to relationships than their suburban counterparts.

Here's the surprising secret—city life is more naturally communal than suburban life. People who live in multifamily dwellings do not have their own backyards—the local park is their backyard. They park their cars in a communal garage or fight for prime parking on the street. They share common experiences that create opportunities for relational bonding that are harder to come by in the suburbs... for example, one night an inebriated couple pulled the fire alarm in the lobby of the high rise building I live in. Within just a few minutes, everyone in the building was standing out on the street in their winter coats hastily pulled on over their jammies. There we stood—with our sleepy eyes, mussed up hair, bad breath in all our glory. One of our neighbors came over to my wife and observed, "Hey, you and I have the same pajamas!" We were a little scared (wondering if our building was going to burn to the ground in front of our eyes) and a lot irritated, but quickly found ways to laugh together about our plight. "The night the drunk couple pulled the fire alarm" is still a topic of laughter and conversation at our building barbecues.

In contrast, when we lived in a single-family house in the suburbs, our smoke alarm went off in the middle of the night and we were the only ones in the neighborhood impacted by the disruption. My point is this: the realities of space and proximity in urban neighborhoods means urban residents tend to naturally share more of life together than people who live in suburban settings. Even single-family home neighborhoods in the city tend to have small houses on small lots, so residents tend to congregate in coffee shops, parks and walkable retail spaces. There is an ongoing sense that we are all in this together. The hallways of my building, the stairs and elevators, the sidewalks and parks are all shared space that I have in common with hundreds of other people. It's really hard to be in an elevator with the same person every day and never acknowledge them. So we live life up close and personal.

Even the layout of suburbs is designed to make a statement that this is mine and that is yours. We mow our grass and know exactly where the line is between our neighbor's grass and our grass. Our property is our property and if you come on to my property uninvited, I have the right to shoot you and literally get away with murder. I did not know the names of the neighbors who lived next door to me for at least three years. We didn't need to know. Suburbs are structured to honor individual rights and private property. Living in the city requires you to get along, or you simply will be unable to stay and/or be miserable.

The communal value of the city lends itself to a crucial opportunity for the Church. Building relational connections with urban neighbors is a very natural endeavor. Because we have so much in common, we start with shared interests that are easy to talk about. The sharing of everyday mundane things like fire alarms lays a foundation for conversations that go deeper. Conversations that go deeper have the potential of becoming spiritual conversations where truth can be shared and spiritual influence can happen.

This is the how of influence. Influence begins with friendship and friendship begins with shared experience and cities are literally designed around shared experience. The greatest impediment to the Church engaging in relationships that influence cultural formation is that the presence of the people of the Church is thin in the city. It may have been Tim Keller who first said, "The greatest need of the city is for the people of the Church to move back into the city." It's not enough to live out on the perimeter of the urban core and react. We've got to rediscover the strategic importance of proactively being present where truth is needed most. The opportunity to move into the neighborhood and build relationships with neighbors is incredibly significant.

FOCUS

Density is an opportunity. The average density of a city neighborhood is about 6,500 souls per square mile. This means that on average 6,500 people live within walkable distance of each other. These 6,500 persons will tend to share a common lived experience. This presents a wonderful opportunity for the Church to focus its ministry toward incarnating the Gospel in language, symbols and actions that will be meaningful to the inhabitants of this particular neighborhood. Instead of standing on a stage and proclaiming that "we are going to take this city!," the density of urban neighborhoods provides a wonderful opportunity to stand on a street corner and proclaim "we are going to do everything we can to make Jesus known to the people who are within easy walking distance of where we now stand."

I am unaware of a single example of a city anywhere in the world where one single church entity is the only place of worship for everyone in the entire city. Joel Osteen fills a Houston stadium every week with perhaps 43,500 people or so, but that means there are over 2 million residents of Houston who are not in his church. The largest church in the world is Yoido Full Gospel Church in Seoul, Korea where over 480,000 gather for worship every week, which means that over 9 million residents of Seoul do not darken the door of Yoido Full Gospel.

Single churches don't win cities. Multiple custom-built, neighborhood-focused churches are how city dwellers are best introduced to Jesus. Multiple hyper-local expressions of the Church are how cities are won.

CREATIVITY

Cities are open to new approaches. The entrepreneurial spirit that makes cities a magnet for young dreamers who hope to become the next Mark Zuckerberg is an incredible opportunity for the Church. Especially new and creative forms of the Church. Stuck, passionless churches that are basically museums to days gone by will not thrive in the rapidly evolving culture of burgeoning cities. Rapid innovation is a valued attribute among the cultural architects of the future.

Thankfully, God is actually the most creative Being in the universe. After all, He spoke the entire universe into existence! So, His Church, guided by the prompting of His Holy Spirit, has the potential to be ahead of the creativity curve of culture. The cultural openness to "what's next" can actually provide an opportunity for the voice of the Church to redemptively address the toughest issues of city living.

Cities are loaded with opportunities for the Gospel to thrive. So why is the Church less present in cities?

Appendix E: Why Is The Church Less Present In Cities?

The world is becoming irreversibly more urban every day. And, despite the challenges cities pose for the Church, cities are full of great opportunities waiting to be leveraged by the Church. So why are there three to four times more local churches per capita in the suburbs than in the cities? Why is the Church less present in cities?

Many of the challenges we've addressed previously are part of the answer to this question. The cost of funding a traditional church is certainly an obstacle to increasing the presence of the Church in city neighborhoods. Urban churches typically encounter higher operating costs, while at the same time experiencing less income. Higher costs combined with less income is not helpful to churches hoping to serve a community over the long haul.

The complicated culture of cities is another reason the Church is missing in action. Increasingly, the political bias in cities leans toward "liberal" and "progressive" stances on social issues that can be at odds with the historic biblical positions. People of the Church living in city neighborhoods find themselves surrounded by actions, attitudes, and viewpoints that they feel compelled to disagree with. The tension can feel exhausting and the right response is not always obvious. Frankly, it's easier to be the Church where the culture appears to be more aligned with prevailing principles of biblical truth.

Another reason the presence of the Church is thin in the urban context is that the most popular methods for starting new churches are mostly ineffective. This happens way too often. A well-meaning suburban church decides to start a church in the city core. They do all the right things according to the most prominent church-starting advocates. The vision is cast, the money is spent, but the result is not what everyone expected. The new church manages to eke out an existence for a while, but eventually, the painful decision is made to close the doors. Most often, this is a financial issue, but regardless of why, the outcome is the same—more people, less church.

Loneliness. Because people willing to start urban churches are relatively rare, they have few actual peers to learn from, compare notes with, and be encouraged by. Sure, they can hang out with the suburban church-planting friends, but they will quickly discover they have very little in common. Additionally, quite often their supervisors are leaders whose primary experience is in the suburban or rural contexts, so it's hard for them to genuinely resonate with the challenges of urban planting. Add on top of all this that the majority of the immediate neighbors of the church planters will be people who have a very low or skewed view of the Church and it all adds up to a serious sense of isolation for the church starter. This sense of isolation begins to wear and tear on the church planter and family. The solution is, for the sake of the family, to go back to the suburban or rural places from which they came. And, once again, more people, less Church.

Metrics. What gets measured gets done. The gold standard of church success has become "noses" and "nickels"—how many people sit in the pew each week to hear you preach and how much money do they put in the offering? The challenge for the vast majority of urban church starters is that both of these numbers will on average be significantly smaller than their suburban counterparts. It's discouraging to go to fellowship meetings and be reminded that your little urban flock is just a fraction of the number of excited people who attend the brand-new big box in the suburbs. Oh and by the way, you've been at it for six years and they just started six months ago. What's wrong with you anyway? Like water, we are all prone to take the path of least resistance, and the temptation to go back where the numbers and bank accounts are big is just too attractive. And so, once again...more people, less church.

I believe all of the aforementioned reasons why the presence of the Church is thin in the city are symptoms of deeper issues that the Church must come to terms with. I'm convinced that unintentionally, over time, the Church has drifted dangerously in some key missional areas. I believe this drift, if allowed to continue, is an existential threat to the viability of the Church that Jesus is building. Here are some of the underlying core issues that are keeping the Church from clearly seeing the urban as a crucial missional focus.

FRACTURED MISSIOLOGY.

Jesus said the people of His Church would be witnesses in Jerusalem, Judea, Samaria, and the whole earth. Many missiologists agree that these four places represent four areas of focus that every church is called to give attention to. Jerusalem refers to reaching people who live near you and are like you. Judea refers to a region composed of people slightly removed from your immediate context but who are similar to you in culture and language.

Samaria refers to people who are somewhat near, but different from you. The whole world refers to people who are far from you and different from you in language and culture. Modern missiology has been fractured into two areas of focus—Jerusalem and the whole world. Billions of dollars are invested annually by local churches to provide an outstanding worship environment and culture for people near them and like them. Billions more are spent on those who are different and far away. But little missional intentionality is exercised toward those who are in Judea and Samaria—people near us and different from us. I would contend that city neighborhoods are the Samaria of the modern-day church.

A broadband approach to missiology would mean that we give missional focus to all four of the sectors of culture that need the attention of the Church. We cannot choose to ignore those who are near us but different from us. It's part of our missional mandate.

Lack of missional clarity. Jesus was once asked to explain why he had come. His answer is crucial in understanding this next core reason the presence of the Church is thin in the city. His answer is that He came to seek and save the lost. That was the mission of Jesus. That is the mission of the Church He is building. Period. A look at the prevailing focus on the modern church looks very different from the mission of Jesus—although we'd never say this out loud, our actions are speaking louder than our words—our mission, based on our actions, appears to be to gather and encourage the found.

LACK OF RETURN ON INVESTMENT.

It pains me to write this, but perhaps the most dire reason the Church is less present in cities is actually a financial one. A shocking article in *The*

Atlantic spells out the problem in no uncertain terms. "Churches are not just faith institutions; they are economic institutions, too. And church life in general seems to be falling along economic lines: Churches of all sizes proliferate in the suburbs and the tonier parts of America's urban cores, while in lower-income, economically stagnant neighborhoods, churches tend to be very small, very old, and in general, not as active in their community.... That's the loop of church economics: It needs money to serve people, but in many cases, it gets that money from the community it serves. So ministers are incentivized to plant and grow their churches in areas where people can afford to give money away."[52] In summary, Patton Dodd is saying that church starters and the organizations that send them are de-incentivized from starting new churches in the harder, underserved, and economically challenged communities because the "return on investment" isn't there.

There are actually quite a few reasons why, in general, as the density of the population goes up, the presence of the Church goes down. But it's fair to ask if this is a real problem or a temporary setback. After all, by all appearances, cities do still have churches present inside the city limits. Shouldn't our strategy be to strengthen what remains? If starting is so expensive, isn't it better stewardship to help the existing congregations thrive? We will look at this question in the next appendix.

APPENDIX F

NOT ENOUGH—
BUT CITIES DO HAVE CHURCHES, RIGHT?

Sometimes it really does feel like the Church has abandoned the city. Here's a quote from a rather disturbing article on *Denverite*. "But actually, one out of every five churches in Denver was part of a sale within the last eight years. And some don't stay churches.

"In Denver, we have churches that have become clubs, churches that have become art galleries, even church churches that have become homes. And the number of churches that have been repurposed is only poised to rise. At one point, churches were the bedrock of American social life, and skylines reflected that with dramatic architecture that punctuated every city landscape. Now, many of those original tenants face mounting operational costs and dwindling congregations."[53]

Be sure you understand what the author is saying here. When she writes the word "church," she is referring to the physical building where the Church

53   https://denverite.com/2017/06/09/
denver-church-sales-new-uses-historic-old-buildings/

has historically gathered for worship, fellowship, and service. But the picture she paints is concerning—it sounds like the Church is in full retreat from being present in the city, as evidenced by the rapid loss of real estate.

The situation in Denver is not an isolated case. In an article in *The Atlantic*, Jonathan Merritt makes the startling observation that "6,000 to 10,000 churches die each year in America." He goes on to write, "Many houses of worship sit on prime real estate, often in the center of towns or cities, where inventory is low. Selling the property to the highest bidder is a quick and effective way to cut losses and settle debts."[54]

While the situation is indeed dire, at this point, the Church has not completely abandoned cities. New urban churches are being started. Existing churches are continuing to exist. So why should we make the investment of people and finances to start more new churches where it seems that increasingly, churches are not wanted? After all, cities do still have some churches. Why aren't they enough? Let's look at the current reality of the church in the city.

A quick internet search of church options in almost any city will yield what appears to be a robust and healthy number of churches sprinkled throughout the metro area. For example, the search for churches inside the city limits of Denver yields the names of 217 churches, which sounds like a lot until you do the math and realize that's one church for every 3,364 residents. The American average of churches per capita is about one church for every 817 Americans. So the average American community may have as many as four times as many churches per capita as an American city. Couple that with the reality that city congregations tend to be smaller in number of attendees, and the picture becomes even more distressed.

---

54   https://www.theatlantic.com/ideas/archive/2018/11/
what-should-america-do-its-empty-church-buildings/576592/

But there are indeed churches in the city, and new churches are being started in the cities. In fact, many aspiring church starters are targeting city neighborhoods, hoping to reverse the downward spiral of the cities. Here's an overview of the types of churches in the city.

TYPES OF CHURCHES IN THE CITY

Existing faithful churches:

I'm genuinely grateful for the faithful congregations that chose to stay in the city when many of their peers moved out to the suburbs. City neighborhoods are indeed sprinkled with these wonderful, tenacious bands of believers who have stayed and are doing their best to continue to shine the Gospel light in a context that is dramatically changing around them. These churches deserve the appreciation and respect of the broader Body of Christ, because in many cases, without these determined Gospel outposts, city neighborhoods would have no local Gospel witness at all.

One might argue that the best strategy for increasing the presence of the Church in the city would be to help these existing churches thrive. While I would certainly agree that we should do everything possible to strengthen and invigorate existing urban churches, even if we are completely successful at turning every existing church into a "powerhouse," the urban challenge will still remain.

Why? Several reasons come to mind. First of all, there simply aren't enough existing churches to meet the missional challenge. We've already observed that the ratio of urban churches to population is far below the general average of church-to-person ratio. Second, many of these existing churches are at a point in their life cycle where they are fighting for survival. They face these existential struggles for a variety of reasons:

changing economic realities, demographic shifts, the increasing average age of the gathered congregants, etc. If the generally accepted stats about churches everywhere are applied to urban churches, we know that about 80 percent are in plateau or in decline—which means that less than 20 percent of the existing urban churches are anywhere near thriving.

So while we celebrate, appreciate, and honor these existing hero churches, there simply aren't enough thriving ones to meet the increasing missional challenge of city neighborhoods.

"Pioneer churches":

These are the hardy souls who have recognized the missional challenge of the urban context and have decided to do something about it. We are super-grateful for these friends who are making Jesus known in urban places, often at great personal sacrifice. These come in a variety of approaches, some more successful than others. However, more often than not, these pioneer churches have been informed by suburban church-starting models that have proven to be ineffective in the urban context. This means that many of these well-intended pioneer start-ups spend a lot of money in a short time but never arrive at a point of sustainability because the assumptions that make suburban church-starting models work are simply not present in the urban context. Many of these pioneers and the organizations who send them, having given it the best shot and not knowing of any different start-up approaches to utilize, retreat back to the familiar ground of the suburbs and the urban residents continue to be underserved by the Church. A handful of these pioneers actually "make it," but the vast majority tend to struggle to survive over the long haul and often require an ongoing stream of "outside" investment to continue to exist. We are grateful for these pioneers, but once again, there are not enough to make a significant impact on the overall spiritual health of the city.

"One-hit wonders":

One-hit wonders are a non-reproducible combination of talent, opportunity, timing, miracle, and perhaps even a little very non-spiritual luck. An example of a one-hit urban wonder might be Pastor Jim Cymbala of Brooklyn Tabernacle in NYC. Pastor Jim is a once-in-a-lifetime mix of anointing, giftedness, tenacity, faith, and other intangibles that God raised up to be a bright light in a great city. We thank God for leaders and churches like Pastor Cymbala and Brooklyn Tabernacle. Cities need more of these kinds of stories and these kinds of leaders. The challenge with one-hit wonders is that they are not reproducible. Even though they do have much to teach us, these kinds of churches are a one of a kind. The set of circumstances that allowed them to emerge is impossible to repeat, which means they don't lend themselves to being reduced to a strategy that can be followed and result in similar outcomes.

Celebrity churches:

Hillsong is one of the better-known examples of this type of church that is currently active in an increasing number of cities. The Hillsong phenomenon is incredible and there is no question that they are adding value to the spiritual well-being of the cities where they go. But like one-hit wonder churches, celebrity churches are not reproducible. Almost by definition, they are one and done in a metro area. You can't start a celebrity church unless you are a celebrity or you have the right to use a celebrity association (Hillsong churches). If the church gathers because of celebrity, then can a city have more than one of that kind of church and the model be effective?

So far, the answer appears to be "No." So while celebrity churches are a positive part of increasing the presence of the Church in the urban context, their ultimate impact is limited due to their inability to reproduce in that local context.

"Cultural churches":

These are churches that gather around language and/or culture. Neighborhoods populated by a high number of immigrants from the same nation of origin are common places for a cultural church to emerge. Larger cities especially are sprinkled with hundreds of these wonderful churches where language and culture are the common ground for worship. Clearly, churches that empower people to worship in their heart language are needed and strategically essential. As the American culture continues to diversify, the need for these specialized culture/language-based churches will continue to grow—at least for the foreseeable future. The obvious limitation for cultural churches is that they are not a good option for people who do not speak the language or understand the culture. So these churches' missional effectiveness is limited by language and culture.

Campus/branch/site:

This occurs when a strong suburban church sees the need in their "Samaria" and decides to do something about it by leveraging their strength to open a location in an urban neighborhood. The location may take the form of an extension campus, video venue, customized church plant, or some other expression that allows the suburban church to have a real presence in the heart of an urban neighborhood. This approach has many, many advantages and may perhaps have the most potential for the kind of exponential impact that is needed in cities. It's reproducible, efficient, effective, and consistent with how the Church has historically moved forward. The problem with this approach is that it is too rare.

Has the Church completely abandoned the cities? Clearly the answer has to be no. Faithful existing churches are in the city. Pioneers continue to be sent to the city. One-hit wonders continue to emerge in the city. Celebrity churches keep starting in the cities. Cultural churches are emerging in the city. Strong suburban churches are starting works in the city. So, no, the cities have not been forgotten by the Church. But the alarming reality in the city is that even with all the worthy efforts that are being made, the Church continues to fall behind. The trend continues to be, as the density of the population goes up, the presence of the Church goes down.

The presence of the Church needs to increase in cities. If we have any hope of seeing the Gospel light push back the growing darkness of our culture, we must make increasing the presence of the Church in the city a top missional priority. It can't be a side effort. It must be central to our ministry strategies and organizational focus. Increasing the Church in the city cannot be simply an afterthought.

The first step to solving this problem is sincerely acknowledging that we have one. We've observed that the recent trend toward urbanism has created a challenge for the Church that has never existed before. We've noted that God loves people and because cities are high concentrations of people, God loves cities. So when we care about cities, we are aligning ourselves with God's concerns. We've recognized that cities are challenging places for the Church to thrive. We've recognized that some noble efforts are being made to address the urban challenge, but they are not enough. Business as usual will not suffice. The purpose of this book is to propose a vision of what *business unusual* will look like!

APPENDIX G

GUIDELINES FOR "REFORMATTING" AN EXISTING CHURCH

Although the main focus of this book is on starting new churches in challenging neighborhoods, the principles are applicable to existing churches everywhere. This appendix contains some suggestions for reformatting your church from a 20th century platform to a platform optimized for the 21st century.

1. **Don't expect to bring everyone along with you.** Reformatting your church for the 21st century starts with healthy expectations. Your temptation will be to stand in front of your congregation and announce that, effective immediately, all current ministries of the church will be discontinued and fantastic new ways of being the church will begin. Expecting an affirmative response to such an announcement would be a prime example of an unhealthy expectation. A healthy and realistic expectation is that despite your best efforts and patient tenacity, some of the people who are currently part of the church will not ever be supporters of the transition from

20th-century to 21st-century modalities. The best you can hope for is that you will be able to help the resisters find a church home that is more in line with their church preferences. Even when resisters moving on goes well, it hurts. Friendship are changed or even lost. Some people will feel that you have stolen "their church" from them. If you aren't ready for some pain, then don't endeavor to reformat your church.

2. **Go with the goers.** Identify people in the congregation who are personally living in a manner that is informed by 21st-century realities. Notice that I did not say identify people who think like you do or agree with you philosophically. Your focus should be on how they are living life —their behavior. You'll know it when you see it because you say to yourself, "I wish everyone in the church lived life like these people do." When you say that about someone, they are a "goer." Once you've identified the goers, it's time to form a guiding coalition, dream team, healthy huddle, etc. Call it whatever you like, but plan on giving at least 50 percent of your time and attention to these "goers."

3. **Continue doing 20th-century church as usual with minimum energy expenditure.** If you are giving 50 percent of your time and energy to the goers, you won't have as much time and energy for the rest of the church attendees. The good news is that passive attendees are mainly concerned that the boat is not rocked. So, preach good sermons, visit them in the hospital, marry, bury, etc. The key is to avoid disrupting the normal habits of the church. The Sunday morning worship experience should stay predictable. Other church ministries should continue to operate as they always have. The key to success in this guideline is to literally do just enough to get by.

4. **Initiate 21st-century practices through the goers.** Invite the goers you have selected into a journey of discovery with you. It's important that this is an invitation-only group and, in the beginning, you are the only person who can invite people to be part of the goers group. It's also best if the goers group is kept "off the radar" of the general church. No bulletin announcements or references from the pulpit or social media. Give the goers space to experiment without judgment or evaluation. The focus of the goers group should be to live out the 21st-century church principles described in this book and begin to understand how those principles should become practices that are contextually relevant and missionally fruitful.

5. **Practice distributed leadership.** Most 20th-century churches were formatted to be led by one strong benevolent leader. Other leaders were enlisted to support and carry out the vision of the key leader. Your goers group is a fantastic opportunity to set in motion a 21st-century distributed leadership approach. As early as possible, invite members of the goers group to catalyze other goers groups. Distributed leaders qualify to lead based on their actual behavior, not the completion of a class or the signing of a pledge. As distributed leaders are activated, the goers group will increase in impact and influence. This will also increase the leadership capacity of the church, which in turn increases the missional options the church is equipped to pursue.

6. **Make everything an experiment.** The goers group will be the place where principles are shaped into practices that will eventually become habits for the reformatted church. Keep the principles

strong and the practices soft until the practices have proven to be appropriate for the context. A great way to keep practices soft until they prove themselves is to call everything an "experiment." An experiment cannot "fail," because it either produces missional results or not. Either way, experiments will allow the goers group to learn together and formulate best practices that will stand the test of the context.

6. **Be willing to send the goers out as a new faith community.** The hoped-for outcome of this process is that eventually, the goers will become the dominant influencers in the church and collectively lead the way to changing the habits of their fellow congregants. The existing church will be reformatted. However, it is possible that the folks who prefer the status quo will resist the changes that the goers seek to put into practice. When this happens, another possible option is for the existing church to send out the goers to start a new faith community built from the start on a 21st-century platform.

7. **Trust the principles—be patient with the process.** The Twelve Shifts described in this book have their foundation in core biblical principles. They have also been field-tested with 40+ new churches starting up in difficult places where 21st-century values are already fully activated. However, reformatting a church is a major undertaking that will not happen overnight. I recently observed an existing church decide to reformat themselves by basically putting lipstick on a pig. They rebranded themselves, mistakenly thinking a new name and fresh coat of paint would result in crowds flocking through their doors. It didn't work. In fact, a year later the church closed its doors

for good. Reformatting that lasts requires much deeper work than a new logo or new set of value statements. It requires the majority of the congregants to significantly modify their behavior. This takes determination and time, especially from those who are leading the reformatting process.

8. **Be mean about the vision.** Existing church reformatting processes are vulnerable to the opinions of stakeholders who like their church "just the way it is, thank you very much." Theologians tell us that Jesus was 100 percent God and 100 percent man at the same time. Church members, on the other hand, are 100 percent man in the process of being conformed to the image of Christ. They are a work in progress. Some of these unfinished masterpieces have been known to act out in all kinds of unhealthy ways to derail reformatting processes they don't like. They gossip, use their money to influence decisions, create division, and, if you're blessed, stomp out the door and shake the dust off their feet. Your vision for a reformatted church will be tried and tested. I don't know where I heard the phrase "Be mean about the vision." But I've found it to be true over the years. To put it another way—don't let the naysayers, detractors, and obstructers cause you to veer away from the vision of a church reformatted for the 21st century. If it doesn't move you toward the God-given goal line, don't do it. Period.

9. **Be committed to the metrics.** One of the most important value-adds in this book are the tools we've introduced for measuring missional progress. We've said it before—what gets measured gets done. If you are seriously committed to successfully leading your church through

a reformatting process, you must select the right metrics to measure your progress. Continuing to use 20th-century metrics (noses and nickels) as your standard of success will cause you to prioritize the wrong behaviors and sabotage your reformatting efforts. Choose metrics that matter and stick with them.

10. **Be transformed by the renewing of your own mind.** One of the major reasons that reformatting efforts fail is that the leaders themselves are not reformatted. We have observed that leaders transitioning from a 20th-century mindset to a 21st-century mindset tend to go through stages of transformation. The longer a leader has led in a 20th-century context, the more challenging the transition will be. This is why it's important to ask yourself why you desire to reformat your church. The only right reason to do so is that you sincerely desire to more effectively be on mission with Jesus. Reformatting efforts motivated by a desire for "church growth" or "keeping up with the most current ministry trends" are doomed to fail. Decide to reformat for the right reason and understand that you yourself will be reformatted through the process.

This list of guidelines is specifically designed to help you deal with the most daunting reformatting obstacle—*human nature*. Humans are hardwired to be creatures of habit. Familiar patterns and habits corporately shared are difficult to change. Every leader seeking to reformat an existing church, especially a long-established one, will inevitably run into the human preference for status quo. The edges of the reformatting trail are littered with the remains of well-intended efforts to lead a group of people through a process of change.

But reformation is possible. A friend of mine was assigned by his denomination to take on the challenge of a church near the end of its life cycle. The church had a decent facility that was paid for. But the congregation had dwindled down to a handful of senior citizens who had neither the vision nor the energy for reformatting the church. After assessing the reality of the situation, my friend decided he had two options. Option 1) Work really hard to inspire his tired little flock to take on the mission of Jesus with renewed vigor. Option 2) Serve the existing congregation as a chaplain and start a new church on the side.

My friend chose Option 2. He kept all of the familiar patterns of the church in place. Every Sunday at 10:45 a.m. (as they had done for decades), the people of the church met for worship. Every Wednesday at 7 p.m. they met for Bible study and prayer. He visited them in the hospital and supported them through weddings and funerals. He devoted about 25 percent of his time and energy into the maintenance side of Option 2.

With the remaining 75 percent of his time and energy, he acted like a church starter. He built relationships with his neighbors, started Alpha Groups for seekers and hosted Bible studies for saints. None of these activities ever took place at the church building. As the various groups outgrew the homes where they met, they moved into a community center for a Tuesday night Bible study and prayer meeting. Soon, it became clear to everyone that a new community of faith was forming. He began to talk with his community center Bible study group about the possibility of recognizing themselves as a church. They liked the idea.

Meanwhile, back at the existing church, he began a series of messages about forming redemptive relationships with neighbors. He announced that in six weeks, the church would be hosting a "Friend Day" when every member would be encouraged to invite their friends to join them for worship. He asked "Betty" to bake three dozen of her famous chocolate-chip cookies. He gave "Fred" a bright orange vest with an equally orange flag on a stick and asked him to direct traffic. His congregants thought he was a little crazy because they had tried stuff like this before and it hadn't made much of a difference. But he had won their hearts and they decided to play along, hoping that the disappointment wouldn't be too hard on him.

Back at the Bible study at the community center, he announced that he had arranged for a place for them to begin meeting on Sundays. He shared the date for their first meeting, which of course, just happened to be the date of the Friend Day back at the existing church building.

Friend Day arrived. The congregants of the existing church showed up with their trays of baked goods wondering what they would do with all the leftovers. Fred showed up carrying his orange flag and wearing his orange vest. He dutifully took up his post in the parking lot, feeling a little silly as he prepared to engage in what he expected to be an exercise in futility. But it wasn't long before he rushed into the foyer announcing to anyone who would listen: "There's a line of cars heading into the parking lot!"

It was on that day that the church was reformatted. The newcomers outnumbered the members of the existing congregation 10 to one. The old-timers were delighted to once again hear the laughter of children echoing up and down the hallways. Of course, a few of the old-timers expressed frustration over the ways that the newcomers had changed "their" church. But the net result was a dying church received an infusion of life.

Reformatting an existing church IS possible. But it is really, really hard.

My friend basically worked two full-time jobs simultaneously to facilitate the reformatting process. This story had a happy ending, but not every reformatting process is blessed with this level of success.

With that in mind, it is worth considering the possibility that starting a new church may be the better option. The advantages of starting a new church are many.

1. The members of the existing church will not need to disturb their familiar habits and patterns of worship, yet they can celebrate the missional success of the new church they sponsored.

2. The new church can be custom designed for the context and people it's meant to serve.

3. The new church can start with a heavy emphasis on missional engagement from the very beginning.

4. The sending church can be intentional about developing a diversified revenue stream strategy to enable the new church to be sustainable right out of the gate.

5. The new church creates new opportunities and ways for people to lead, serve, and worship.

6. The new church can be started with an embedded DNA of multiplication.

7. Churches that are intentional about multiplication have been shown to be healthier, stronger, and more missionally effective over the time.

I could likely list at least 20 more benefits of starting a new church. It may be wise to consider the possibility that the best way to reformat your church is to leave the existing church as it is and focus on starting new ones.

ABOUT THE AUTHOR

Steve Pike is the President and Founder of Urban Islands Project, a national organization dedicated to increasing the presence of the Church in North America's urban and underserved communities.

Prior to initiating Urban Islands Project, Steve served as the Founding Director of the Church Multiplication Network. CMN serves church multipliers to equip, fund and network new faith communities in America. Since its formation in 2008, CMN has assisted with the starting of over 4000 new congregations in every region of the US.

Steve is the co-author with Dr. Tom Nebel of "Leading Church Multiplication," which has become the "go to" book for denominational and network church multiplication leaders. He is also the author of "Total Fitness for Your Church.".

Steve works co-vocationally as a coach/consultant with Church Multiplication Partners, providing support denominational and network level church multiplication leaders.

He also serves as a consultant/coach with The Answer Group, a business consulting company.

Steve's passion for church multiplication began in 1989 when Steve and his wife, Cherri, pioneered a new church that became the catalyst of a church planting movement in the state of Utah that continues to this day. The Pikes make their home in Denver, Colorado. They are blessed to be the parents of Lindsy and Jeremy and the grandparents of Myles, Koen and Wesley.

The problem with best practices
is that by the time they are discovered
and developed into training programs,
culture has moved on and
the 'best practices' are no longer 'best.'
What is needed is a learning community
made up of practitioners
who are learning together
in real time.

-Len Sweet

WANT TO JOIN AN ONGOING CONVERSATION WITH LEADERS DOING MINISTRY IN HARD PLACES WORLDWIDE?

JOIN US FOR CONVERSATION, RESOURCES, AND BEST PRACTICES AT NEXTWAVE.COMMUNITY.

Made in the USA
Middletown, DE
31 March 2021